The Stealth Story

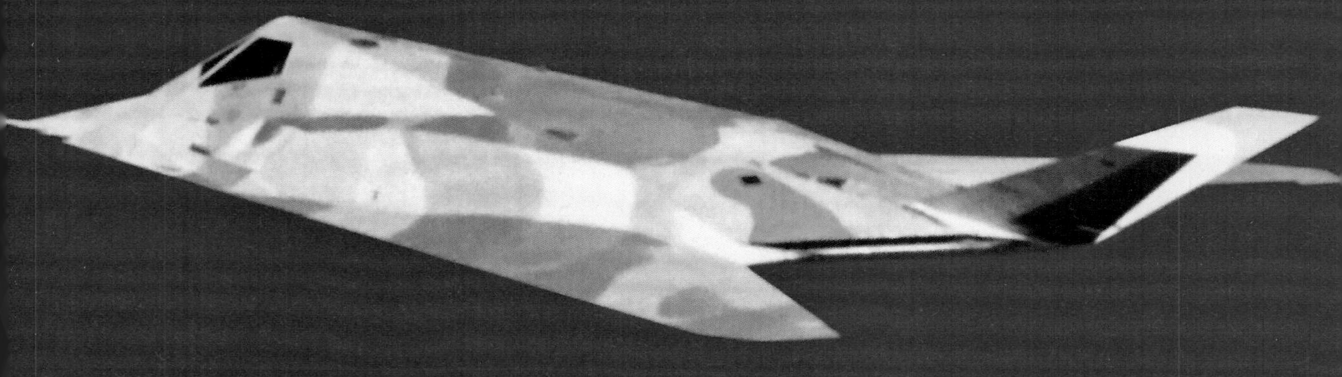

The Stealth Story

Peter R. March

Sutton Publishing

Also in this series:

The Concorde Story

The Spitfire Story

The Vulcan Story

The Red Arrows Story

The Harrier Story

The Dam Busters Story

The Hurricane Story

First published in the United Kingdom in 2007 by
Sutton Publishing, an imprint of NPI Media Group Limited
Cirencester Road · Chalford · Stroud · Gloucestershire · GL6 8PE

British Library Cataloguing in Publication Data
A catalogue record for this book is available from the British Library.

Hardback ISBN 978-0-7509-4486-1

Typeset in Syntax.
Typesetting and origination by
NPI Media Group Limited.
Printed and bound in England.

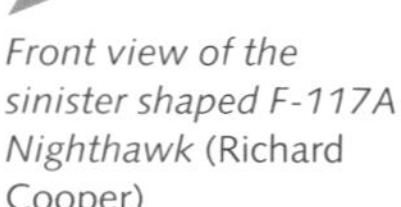

Front view of the sinister shaped F-117A Nighthawk (Richard Cooper)

CONTENTS

The secretive story of Lockheed's Stealth from its inspired conception, through its origination, development, hidden night flying over the Nevada Desert and the F-117's emergence into the daylight seven years after its first flight, is as unusual as its revolutionary appearance. Sorting through the hearsay, deliberate misinformation, anecdotal evidence and the experiences of people involved is as fascinating as any good detective story. Many books have been written on the subject and I am grateful to the authors for providing so much detail, but that in itself has made the task of producing a straightforward account rather more difficult. I would therefore like to thank Brian Strickland for his patient research and Ben Dunnell for helping to sort the wheat from the chaff.

There were clearly going to be gaps in the photographic record, especially through the early 'dark' years. This book would not have been possible without the considerable help given by Lockheed Martin Photographic Department at Palmdale. I would also like to thank Richard Cooper, Jamie Hunter, Andrew March, Daniel March and Frank Mormillo for the outstanding images that they have provided.

Peter R. March

Photo credits

Peter R. March/PRM Aviation Collection, US Air Force and Lockheed-Martin unless otherwise credited.

No aircraft has been designed to meet the same criteria as the Lockheed F-117 Nighthawk. Planned, built and, in its earliest days, operated in the greatest secrecy, the aircraft proved able to penetrate deep into enemy territory at night, without detection and deliver precision-guided munitions with pin-point accuracy. The overriding factor in the design of the airframe was to make it almost 'invisible' to radar. In addition, the

The design of the airframe was to make it almost 'invisible', particularly at night. (Frank Mormillo)

➤
The use of 'stealth technology' made detection by enemy radar almost impossible.

➤➤
Flat faceted sections scattered the interrogating radar energy.

aircraft has a much reduced heat signature, reduced acoustic output and low electro-magnetic signature, making its detection by enemy forces almost impossible.

To bestow the aircraft with its 'stealthiness', the F-117 was carefully designed with flat faceted sections to scatter the interrogating radar energy from enemy sources, thereby giving the aircraft its unique 'angular' appearance. Aerodynamically unstable, the 'stealth' is controlled by a 'fly-by-wire' control system. The General Electric F404 non-afterburning turbofans give the aircraft a low noise signature and are exhausted through specially designed 'platypus' flattened, louvre-type ducts made of a honeycomb sandwich of nickel alloy, to absorb much of the engines' heat. The engine nozzles are not visible from anywhere beneath the aircraft, again

Did you know?

All aircraft have a 'radar signature' that allows them to be detected by radar. Radars work by the transmission of energy waves as they reflect off an object. The reduction of the aircraft's radar cross-section (RCS) to levels that would provide a significant operational advantage, had been the 'holy grail' for military designers for decades.

helping to reduce the heat signature. These measures to ensure stealthiness ultimately affect the F-117's overall performance. At maximum take-off weight, the aircraft's thrust-to-weight ratio is less than a Jaguar and, in 'hot and high' climates, the take-off roll is long and the climb rate is sluggish.

The F-117 was not designed to be able to tangle with enemy fighters or outrun and outmanoeuvre them in combat. Its popular 'Stealth Fighter' name, and the 'F' designation, is something of a misnomer, as the jet is, in fact, a small stealth bomber. There was never a requirement for it to shoot down enemy aircraft, nor perform fighter-bomber types of attack on or near the battlefield. It is not a pilot's aeroplane in the same way as an F-16, Jaguar or Hawk. It was designed to meet a specific set of threats and much attention was given to

make its employment in combat as easy as possible for the pilot.

The aircraft's capability is brought to bear by its advanced avionics and systems, unique low-observability and, most importantly, by mission planning. The Nighthawk relies on the most up-to-date reconnaissance and intelligence information to plan its routes to and from the target and execute the

Specially designed 'platypus' ducts absorbed much of the engine's exhaust heat.

The GE F404 turbofan nozzles are not visible from below.

➤➤
The pilot sits on a standard ACES II ejection seat under a heavy-framed canopy. (Richard Cooper)

➤
Maximum weight 'hot and high' take-off roll and climb rate is sluggish.

mission. The success largely depends on the quality of this mission planning. The pilot is responsible for getting the aircraft from 'a' to 'b' in the most efficient and risk-free way. The F-117 has an advanced autopilot, which helps relieve much of the workload, but as a Nighthawk pilot explained: 'I'm still the operator and I'm the guy that makes that aeroplane do what it's meant to do. There are complex procedures and methods to make the plane perform as advertised. You don't just walk out there with a brick, plug it in and away it goes.'

'Make things black and skunky
– that is secretly and smartly.'

Ben R. Rich, head of the Lockheed
Advanced Development Company
'Skunk Works'.

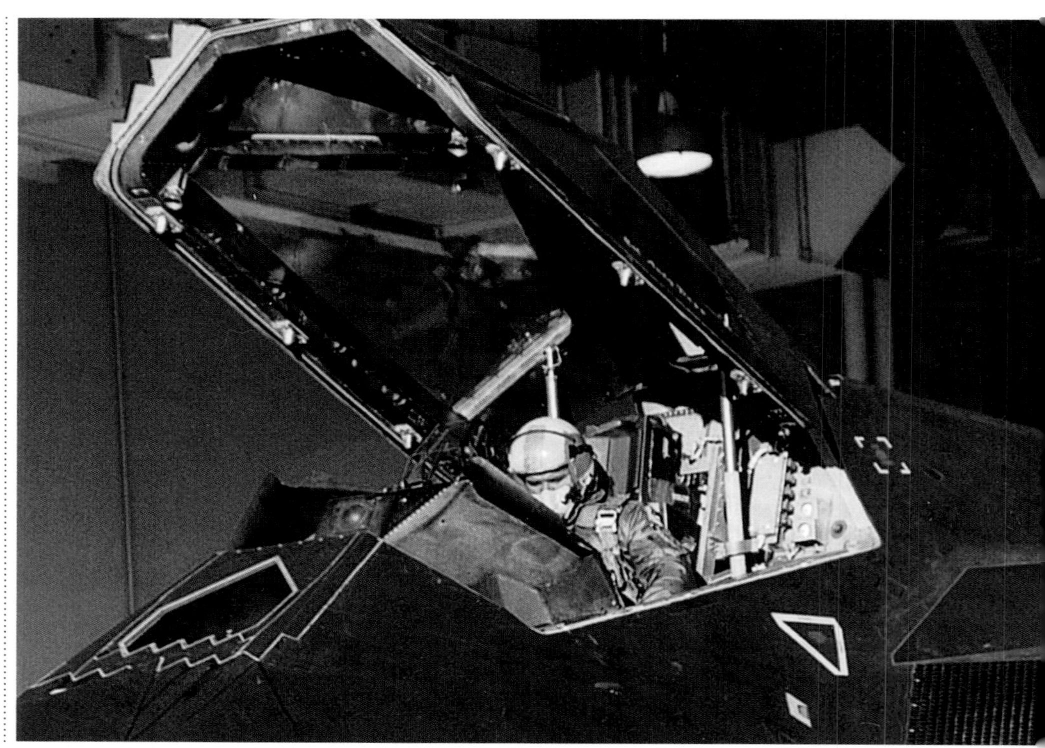

➤
Complex procedures give a heavy workload to the pilot. (Jamie Hunter)

The Second World War demonstrated that air power could play an even more vital part in military operations than had previously been imagined. It also demonstrated the potential of radar, then being developed, as a primary means of detecting aircraft and directing fire against them. Post-war, with the onset of the Cold War, defensive missiles – both ground-launched and air-launched – were developed and 'married' with radar fire control systems. This substantially increased the effectiveness of air defence systems, shifting the balance against aircraft.

In the Cold War, the Soviets placed every emphasis on the development and deployment of air defence missiles in an attempt to offset the advantage the United States had in air power. They built thousands of surface-to-air missile systems, and employed radars with high power and monopulse tracking circuits which were very difficult to jam. Later, they developed air-to-air missiles guided by 'look-down' radars which were capable of tracking aircraft in 'ground clutter'.

Work on stealth-optimised (or low-observable) aircraft had been ongoing for a considerable period of time before the 1980 announcement of the F-117. The invisible weapon has always been the dream of military planners, and the F-117 – the so-called 'Stealth Fighter' – was the first operational platform to come close to realising those dreams.

The ever-increasing surface-to-air missile barrier in the Cold War led to greater interest in low radar cross-section (RCS) and radar-absorbent material (RAM) technology. This was in addition to conventional

Did you know?

The F-117 is perhaps the most unusual looking aircraft ever flown – but its strange shape serves a vital purpose, to make it virtually invisible to radar.

electronic countermeasures. With RAM-type structural elements called corner reflectors, they reflected energy like any other metal surface, the difference being that their triangular configuration created a very effective energy trap.

One of the elements in masking an aircraft's presence lies in controlling its infrared (IR) signature – its acoustic signature and its exhaust emissions. Infrared radiation is electromagnetic radiation with a dual quality. Radar-countering techniques, usually referred to as electronic countermeasures (ECM), are now readily found on virtually all combat aircraft, and are also applicable to other military hardware as well. These can be divided into two broad but basic categories: passive and active. Passive involves the utilisation of the physical characteristics of the aircraft to mask, within limits, its actual visibility, radar cross-section, active emissions such as electronic and infrared, and any other aspect that would reveal its presence to an enemy. Active can involve the use of systems that actively jam, deceive, or in any other way physically inhibit the enemy's ability to locate and destroy its target via electronic means. The two disciplines, when combined, are referred to as defensive ECM.

Lockheed's 'Skunk Works' embarked on a concerted effort to become the industry authority on foiling radar. It became deeply involved with what is known today as 'stealth' or very low-observable (VLO) techniques. Lockheed, with the knowledge that curved surfaces returned considerably less energy to a radar receiver than flat ones, embarked on the first successful RCS. The F-117 was optimised to create

A V-shaped tail has slab 'ruddervators' combining the functions of the rudder and elevator.

Did you know?

The engine intakes are covered with a grill to shield the compressor face from radar. The mesh has to be fine enough to reflect radar, yet wide enough to still allow free passage of air for the engines.

➤ *Located side-by-side, the bomb bays feature one-piece doors opening inwards from a hinge on the centreline.*

the smallest radar target possible that is virtually impossible to track by radar in a combat scenario.

The F-117 has a unique multi-faceted (with angled flat surfaces) shape to minimise radar returns. Its engine gases mix with bypass air and exit through 'platypus' shielded exhausts to dissipate heat emissions and reduce the IR signature. The V-shaped tailplane comprises upper

section slab ‘ruddervators’ that combine the functions of the rudder and elevator. Key surfaces are coated with RAM and composite materials are widely used to absorb unreflected radar energy. Weapons are carried internally, with the Nighthawk’s bomb doors only opening momentarily to release its warload.

With the F-117, Lockheed went to great lengths to ensure that the aircraft’s IR

One of the test aircraft dropping a laser guided bomb during separation trials.

signature was kept to an absolute minimum. Exhaust gases are mixed with relatively cool ambient air in a plenum just aft of the engine compartment. The cooling air is taken in via ducting that brings it from slots located in front of the intakes. After mixing, the exhaust is passed through a horizontal slot-type nozzle assembly that is 6ft wide and some 6in deep. When the gases pass into the aircraft's slipstream, temperature levels have been lowered significantly and the exhaust plume presents a minimal IR target. In addition, the aircraft has a reduced acoustic output.

Theories were verified by Lockheed with radar tests around Groom Lake, Nevada, and the nearby Nellis AFB test ranges, some of which included captured samples of Soviet radar systems. These found that the test aircraft were very difficult to locate and track. If evasive tactical manoeuvres were utilised, the aircraft was almost 'invisible'.

The cooling air is taken via ducting from slots located in front of the intakes. (Richard Cooper)

'They say that if an aeroplane looks right, it will fly right. The F-117 is apparently the exception which proves the rule, possessing admirable handling characteristics.'

Bill Park, Lockheed senior test pilot.

With the shape of the F-117, Lockheed focused on lowering the radar cross-section (RCS), placing heavy emphasis on two major techniques: the use of radar-absorbent material (RAM) and the idea that energy reflected away from a radar's receiver is the same as energy that has been absorbed and/or dissipated.

Lockheed made the first use of stealth design and materials on the Mach 3 SR-71A Blackbird reconnaissance aircraft.

Stealth technology itself had been developed in many experimental programmes, most of them classified, since the immediate post-Second World War period. Shaping techniques and radar-absorbent materials had been successfully used on the Lockheed SR-71 Blackbird, but the development of a tactical stealth aircraft, which would have to operate at lower altitudes in closer proximity to SAMs, required a larger RCS reduction.

Such technology began in nineteenth-century Britain, where Scottish physicist James C. Maxwell derived a set of mathematical formulae to predict the manner in which electromagnetic radiation would scatter when reflected from a given geometrical shape. The questions were further defined by the famous electromagnetic scientist Arnold J. Sommerfeld. In the 1960s, the chief scientist at the Moscow Institute of Radio Engineering, Dr Pyotr Ufimtsev, revisited the Maxwell-Sommerfeld work and simplified it to concentrate on the electromagnetic currents at the edge of geometric shapes.

Today's 'Stealth Fighter' traces its roots to 1974 when the US Defense Advanced Research Project Agency (DARPA) asked five major military aircraft manufacturers to study the potential for developing fighter aircraft with significantly reduced radar detectability. Reducing this had been a priority of Lockheed's Advanced Development Programs (ADP) unit, better known as the 'Skunk Works', for some time.

A retired Lockheed mathematician, Bill Schroeder, proposed that by reducing a three-dimensional body to a finite number of two-dimensional surfaces, the overall radar dissipation patterns could be forecast, and kept to a minimum. The outcome was 'faceting' – creating a three-dimensional aircraft, not out of smooth, gracefully curved surfaces, but a collection of flat panels.

As a result Lockheed's designers produced a shape composed entirely of flat plates, aligned so that they were, at almost all times, angled away from the radar beam in two dimensions. RAM can be fabricated from a wide range of materials. Sheet RAM usually consists of a base, such as rubbers, silicones and polyurethanes, impregnated with materials with magnetic properties, such as carbons, dielectrics and ferrous materials. The molecular structure of all RAM is tailored to absorb as much of the incoming radar energy as possible by

Did you know?

The F-117 flies on the 'lifting body' principle. The undersurface is essentially flat in the central area, but faceting does occur in conjunction with wing and fuselage node lines. Its aerofoil is totally unconventional.

➤
The dramatic wing sweep angles dissipate energy very efficiently and are repeated on all other surfaces.

➤➤
Letterbox-like exhausts allow jet gases to cool rapidly thereby reducing the risk of being picked up by infrared sensors.

Did you know?
Glazing on the F-117 has gold film laminate to lower radar returns from the cockpit area. Also the FLIR-Laser designator unit has gold screen material for protection.

converting it to heat. The F-117 employs RAM on external surfaces and chisel-edge, angular features which contribute to reduced RCS. RAM makes the F-117 dim to radar, while the facets cause it to 'glitter' irregularly as its aspect angle varies.

A basic principle behind low-RCS design is that a flat plate has both the largest and smallest RCS of any simple shape. If the plate is normal to a radar beam, its RCS is enormous. But if it is rotated away from the beam in one dimension, its RCS is far smaller, and if it is rotated in two dimensions (rotated and canted) its RCS is minute. For this reason, the F-117's surface is made up entirely of canted flat plates, or facets. The aircraft's exterior is designed to absorb as many radar signals as possible and deflect the remainder to everywhere except back to the sending antenna.

Did you know?
Conventional aircraft have a large number of elements, such as the tailplanes, wings, engine intakes, fin and rudder that reflect radar echoes back to the transmitting source. This situation is magnified considerably when aircraft have bombs, missiles and auxiliary fuel tanks hanging from external pylons. The F-117 has none of these external appendages.

▲ The fins were carefully angled to help shield the aircraft from infrared sensors, especially those carried by an enemy fighter.

▲ ➤ Glazed cockpit panels are coated with gold. (Daniel J. March)

Letterbox-like exhausts allow jet gases to cool rapidly and thus reduce the risk of being picked up by infrared sensors. The dramatic wing sweep angles (which continue the leading edge lines established by the triangular nose section, something done for stealth, not speed, since the F-117 is subsonic) dissipate energy very effectively and are repeated on all other surfaces; the aircraft's tail fins are not upright, but canted over at an angle, and even the landing gear doors have a serrated profile to reduce radar reflection. Glazed panels are coated with gold to conduct radar energy into the airframe. The RAM is sensitive to moisture and fuel leaks, so F-117 pilots try to keep the aircraft as dry as possible. Most of the structure is made up of aluminium alloys, but some plastic composites are incorporated.

Subsequently, a very different aircraft was tested in secret that demonstrated further steps forward in stealth technology. On 5 February 1982, Lockheed's rival Northrop flew its *Tacit Blue* prototype from Groom Lake, Nevada. *Tacit Blue* was the first aircraft to demonstrate low RCS by using curved surfaces. It also showed how to mount and operate a radar on stealthy aircraft. Officially its main purpose was to explore possibilities of low-speed, long-endurance, stealthy radar surveillance aircraft. Resembling an upside-down bath-tub with stubby wings and a V-tail, *Tacit Blue* was flown 135 times from Groom Lake. Ultimately, the concept was not pursued, and the sole *Tacit Blue* is now displayed in the National Museum of the USAF.

'Fly-by-Wire would even permit the Statue of Liberty to fly.'

Ben R. Rich, head of Lockheed Advanced Development Company 'Skunk Works', previously deputy to Clarence L. 'Kelly' Johnson, founder and leader of the 'Skunk Works'.

Northrop's Tacit Blue *stealth concept aircraft that is now displayed at the National Museum of the US Air Force.*

In August 1975, Lockheed and Northrop were invited to develop and test an aircraft known as the Experimental Survivable Testbed (XST). To validate the 'stealth' approach, a simple aircraft model, nicknamed the 'Hopeless Diamond' by its creators, was built and tested at the 'Skunk Works' electromagnetics facility at Burbank, California. Its radar cross-section proved to be far lower than that of any shape Lockheed had previously trialed. Pole-mounted radar signature models were tested and in April 1976, under the project designation *Have Blue*, Lockheed was declared the winner of the Defense Advanced Research Project Agency (DARPA) competition.

About 40 per cent smaller than the F-117, the XSTs validated the faceting concept on the basic aircraft shape. Key differences between the XST and the F-117

➤ *Pole-mounted, Lockheed's XST model was tested at the RATSCAT range at White Sands, New Mexico.*

that emerged were the inward cantering of the fins, which were mounted on the outside of the main fuselage body, and their positioning much further forward than on the later production aircraft. The all-important leading edge was set at the very sharp angle of 72.5 degrees.

A pair of subsonic *Have Blue* sub-scale proof-of-concept demonstrator aircraft were completed very quickly at Burbank.

The Have Blue *XST was 40% smaller than the F-117 and had inward canted tails.*

The second Have Blue *at Burbank before being flown to the test site in a C-5 Galaxy.*

These were small, piloted, twin-engined technology demonstrators for more extensive flight and RCS testing. Power was from two 2,950lb st (13.12kN) General Electric J85-GE-4A engines, which had come from North American T-2B Buckeye trainers. Although both XSTs crashed, they were deemed a success. Their performance led to a full-scale engineering development contract award for the 'Stealth Fighter' on 16 November 1978.

Did you know?
The F-117's first flight, on 18 June 1981, took place in daylight.

First flight test F-117 #780 on the assembly line early in 1980.

➤ By autumn 1980 #780 had its wings and tail fitted.

➤➤ Before being transported to the flight test site, the F-117's shape was disguised under a timber frame that was securely wrapped.

Results showed such a breakthrough in stealth technology that the unclassified DARPA programme immediately became a 'Black' project. Security was tightened by transferring administration of the programme from the largely civilian-staffed DARPA to the Special Projects Office of the USAF. Under a blanket of security rivalling the 1940s Manhattan Project (which produced the first atomic bombs), Lockheed's team set to work finalising the design and systems for the revolutionary aircraft.

The full-scale production version of the original Lockheed design was developed for the USAF under the programme codename *Senior Trend*. The aircraft was known as this for much of its development and early operational career, shrouded in the utmost secrecy. A production programme began, with the first of five development F-117s being secretly transported to the test site. There were no prototypes, as the first five aircraft were built as flight test vehicles. Lockheed's Hal Farley flew the first of these pre-series F-117s (#780) from Groom Lake on 18 June 1981, a mere thirty-one months after the production go-ahead.

Costs and timetables were kept to a minimum by using numerous 'off-the-shelf' components whose reliability was already proven. These included items such as the F/A-18 Hornet's General Electric F404 very low bypass turbofans (without afterburners), flight controls from the F-16 Fighting Falcon, air-conditioning from a C-130 Hercules, cockpit displays (including head-up display) and control stick from the Hornet and the same aircraft's composite construction technology. The primary sensor display came from the P-3C Orion and OV-10D Bronco. Other parts came from

The first F-117 #780 taxies out of its hangar on 18 June 1981 for its maiden flight.

#780 being prepared for its first flight early in 1981 at the test site.

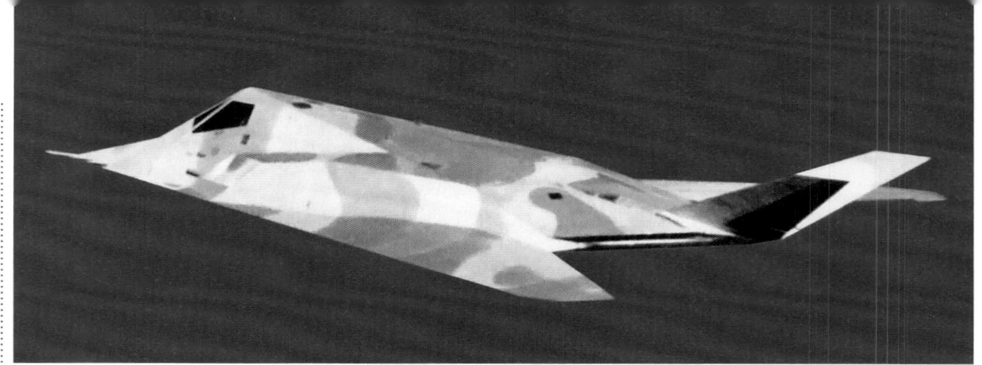

The first F-117 in its unique camouflage during an early test flight. This paint scheme was only used on the first ten flights of the programme undertaken in daylight.

F-117 #780 after being painted in the initial standard light grey overall.

Did you know?

Pilots and the press referred to the F-117 at various times as the *Wobbly Goblin*, *Bat Jet* and *Blue Maria* – but *Nighthawk* became the adopted nick-name.

Did you know?

Once an F-117 airframe was completed at Lockheed's Burbank facility it had to be transported to Tonapah in a Lockheed C-5 Galaxy transport aircraft. First the wings were removed and wooden framework was added around the nose and aft fuselage. The airframe was then wrapped in a large shroud to prevent any uncleared personnel from guessing its true shape while it was being loaded into the awaiting C-5.

the veteran P-2 Neptune, F-104 Starfighter, T-33 and SR-71. Dials, lights and switches date from the analogue features of the 'Century Series' of USAF fighters.

The forward turbine fans of the engines had to be hidden behind special air intake grills to block and disperse radar energy. Other unique screen-grids were designed to allow the aircraft's two 'night-vision' infrared turrets (FLIR and DLIR) to 'see out' without 'being seen' by radar. All doors and removable panels on the aircraft have

Grey-painted #782 had 'stars and stripes' painted on its underside and a black topside for the flypast in November 1983, following which all F-117s were painted black overall.

Did you know?
In order to lower development costs, the avionics, fly-by-wire systems, and other parts are derived from the F-16 Fighting Falcon, F/A-18 Hornet and F-15E Strike Eagle. The parts were originally allocated on budgets for these aircraft, to keep the F-117 project secret.

saw-toothed forward and trailing edges, engineered to direct radar reflections away from the energy source.

This aircraft was initially painted in desert camouflage to distort its faceting, since most flight testing was conducted during daylight hours. No other F-117 was ever painted in this manner. Within a few months, Lockheed standardised on a grey livery for flight test aircraft, but then the USAF directed that all Nighthawks be painted black.

One exception in the early years of the programme was the third Full-Scale Development (FSD) aircraft, serial 79-0782, which had US flag colours painted on its underside for a flypast at the ceremony that unveiled the F-117 to senior US military officials at Groom Lake in November 1983.

'They offered me a chance to fly the F-117 with a new unit, and said it would be top secret. Also that it would require constant separation from my family – and they could not tell me much more. I was given five minutes to make up my mind. They said when I walked through the door my decision stood. It was six years before I could tell my wife.'

Lt Col 'Al' Whitley. A highly decorated combat veteran.

A specially selected, remote and isolated austere base in the high desert just outside Tonopah, Nevada, was developed in the early 1980s as the home of the 4450th Tactical Group. Situated 140 miles north-west of Las Vegas and Nellis AFB (to which the new group would be 'formally' assigned), it was previously used to support nuclear weapons test-related activities. A whirlwind construction programme quickly

Did you know?

A pilot was not allowed to tell his family about his 'bandit number', a secret identity awarded to each man who had flown the F-117.

The Tonopah Test Range in Nevada, located some 140 miles north-west of Las Vegas, was the desert home for the F-117s.

Each aircraft had its own hangar at Tonopah.

Did you know?

Airmen returning to their families in the Nellis-Las Vegas area commuted home on civilian Boeing 727 jetliners operated by Key Airlines – and flown by specially cleared pilots, so once they got back to base they would 'catch the Key home – and go to bed'.

began to transform the landing strip into a modern Air Force Base.

Security was paramount, the base being staffed with USAF security police, and special intrusion monitoring was installed around the perimeter. Each F-117A had its own fully-equipped hangar awaiting its arrival. New buildings were erected and dormitories featured especially effective curtains to block out the sun during daylight sleeping hours. Entry into flightline areas required an electronic palm print scan. Personnel and staff commuted weekly from Nellis AFB aboard a chartered commercial Boeing 727. Moving some 5,000 passengers weekly, the airlift earned the distinction of being the third busiest in the USAF. Everyone stationed at Tonopah learned to live in two worlds, balancing a 'normal' weekend lifestyle with a strict night-time existence from Monday to Friday. High-intensity training quickly honed the skills and confidence of each pilot. Nothing about the aircraft was revealed in public, although by the mid-1980s rumours were rife of a secret 'stealth' aircraft flying by night in the skies of Nevada. Only US personnel who had top security clearances were allowed to know that the aircraft existed – and even then on a 'need to know' basis only.

The purpose of the 4450th Tactical Group was to bring into the world a new kind of aeroplane so revolutionary that not even its existence was admitted. For seven years from 1981, all flying took place at night – the project and 59 production F-117As remained hidden from public view. The cover story was that the group was formed to test A-7 Corsair II avionics, although the USAF's A-7s were by then actually leaving the active duty inventory.

By 1988, the programme had matured to the point that operations could no longer be limited to the dark of night within the highly restricted airspace. Announcing the existence of the programme provided numerous advantages, especially as it allowed a sorely-needed expansion into

Did you know?

By holding fast to the stealthy jet's secrets long after its existence became known, the USAF ensured that even highly informed outside observers had only a vague idea of how well Lockheed and the USAF had succeeded in developing an aircraft that was practically invisible to radar.

Did you Know?

Before flying an operation, each pilot would pick up a letter from the TAC Director of Operations, a two- or three-star general, for use in the event of a diversion to another base. This demanded cooperation from the base commander and his subordinates – telling them to obey the requests and instructions of the bearer, and not to ask any questions.

daylight training exercises. This included multi-force training exercises such as *Red Flag*, as well as integration of the F-117A into overall USAF strategic planning. Following the public announcement of the programme when a grainy photograph was released in November 1988, Tonopah activity then increased with round-the-clock flying.

One of the major obstacles to early training was the lack of F-117A aircraft or even an F-117A flight simulator. The unit did however have a number of A-7 Corsair IIs, and these were used for training flights as delivery of the new 'Black Jets' was awaited. A-7s continued to supplement training while the F-117A inventory grew, but in September 1989 they were replaced by T-38s.

Plans were for 100 F-117As to be built, but budget constraints meant that only 59 were supplied between 23 August 1982 and 12 July 1990, at a total cost of $4,270m. A further $2,000m went on

A-7D Corsairs were assigned to the 4450th Tactical Group for use as covert trainers for F-117 pilots.

Following the move to the Tonopah Test Range, A-7Ds were replaced by Northrop T-38s.

Badge worn by crews of the 415th Tactical Fighter Squadron 'Nightstalkers'.

Did you know?

Initial pilot training took place on Vought A-7D Corsairs and subsequently on Northrop T-38As and AT-38A Talons, during daylight hours. These were followed by preliminary hops out to a radius of 200 miles from Tonopah in the F-117 at night.

research and development and $295m on infrastructure, the latter including 54 individual 'hangarettes' at Tonopah Test Range (TTR), home of the type's initial operating unit, the 4450th Tactical Group.

When the need had passed for a shadowy operating unit, the F-117A began to emerge into the daylight on 5 October 1989, when the 37th Tactical Fighter Wing was re-formed at Tonopah as a regular component of Tactical Air Command. Its three squadrons were the 415th Tactical Fighter Squadron 'Nightstalkers', the 416th TFS 'Ghostriders' and the 417th Tactical Fighter Training Squadron 'Bandits'. The

Did you know?

All F-117 flight operations from Tonopah were conducted at night. There were special precautions, such as keeping the aircraft hangar-bound until 30 minutes after sunset, and ground operations were conducted in blacked-out conditions.

two regular squadrons were assigned 20 F-117As each, while the 417th also operated eight Northrop AT/T-38 Talons for training purposes.

The F-117As were accommodated in individual hangars, arranged in two parallel rows alongside the TTR runway. Constructed from corrugated sheet steel, the shelters were camouflaged in pale sandy pink, marked only by a small black

Hangar lights were switched off before the doors were opened and the F-117 taxied for take-off. (Richard Cooper)

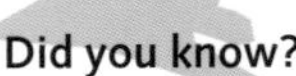

Did you know?

One of the earliest names for the F-117 was *Scorpion*. Apparently, during testing a scorpion found its way into one of the hangars (some sources say onto the programme manager's desk). The Baja Scorpion (Baja for Southern Groom – the F-117s were in the southern hangars of the base) was adopted as the mascot. The scorpion symbol was also used in conjunction with the Dragon Test Team, symbolising that it had remained a symbol for all F-117 flight testing.

Taxying out of the hangar, the pilot viewed the route to the runway using the F-117's FLIR/HUD/IRADS. (Richard Cooper)

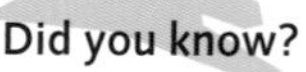

Did you know?

Until the USAF released a single, distorted, dark and grainy photo of the F-117 on 10 November 1988, the existence of the stealth fighter was virtually unknown although it had been flying for more than seven years.

number board. The main doors remained shut until official twilight (defined as half-an-hour after 'official' sunset). Weather and lighting had a disproportionate effect on F-117A operations, with snow, a full moon or unbroken high cloud preventing aircraft from flying 'off-range'. Even 50 per cent moonlight severely restricted the choice of 'off-range'. The threat of hail always kept aircraft firmly grounded, and the earliest F-117As, which did not have heated pitot probes, could not fly if icing was predicted.

The hangar lights would normally be extinguished before the doors were opened, and the pilot would then taxi forward, using the FLIR picture in the head-up display (HUD) (provided by the IRADS – Infrared Acquisition and Designation Systems – sensor) to pick his way through the darkness. Guidance was by groundcrew with electro-lumescent wands, and taxiing was radio-silent and without lights, or simulating A-7 radio calls and callsigns. Take-off clearance could be given by a visual signal, or by radio.

'The F-117 isn't a pilot's aeroplane in the same way as a Jaguar or a Hawk. The aircraft is brought to bear by advanced avionics and systems, unique low-observable capabilities and, most important of all, mission planning.'

Sqn Ldr Richie Matthews RAF, F-117 exchange pilot.

The engines are aspirated through four-sided intakes which are covered by a fine mesh.

The two General Electric F404-GE-F1D2 engines (delivering 10,800lb st/48kN) are buried deep within the fuselage, and are derived from the standard turbofans used on the F/A-18 Hornet. Typically for modern jet engines, the F404 has a basically uncluttered external appearance. Without an afterburner, the engine is remarkably compact. The engines are aspirated through four-sided intakes which are covered by a fine mesh, and fed via curved air intakes so that the highly 'unstealthy' engine compressor faces are hidden from radar. Necessary holes in the shape of the engine intakes and the two Infrared Acquisition and Designation

Efflux from the circular-section jet-pipe mixes with cool bypass air before exiting through a wide, thin slot.

Did you know?

Each aircraft carries a small radar reflector in a prominent position just aft of the 'star-and-bar'. This is necessary in peacetime operations to allow the aircraft to show up on air traffic control screens.

Systems (IRADS) and attack sensors are covered with a grill.

In order to greatly reduce its infrared signature, the F-117A uses a novel slot exhaust. Jet efflux from the circular-section jetpipe is mixed with cool bypass air to cool it, and then widened and flattened to exit the exhaust slot. This is known as the 'Coanda' effect.

Fuel is contained in large tanks situated in the main fuselage body, filling the vacant upper areas fore and aft of the weapons bay. This can be augmented by fuel tanks in the weapons bay for ferry flights. In-flight refuelling is accomplished via a receptacle aft of the fuselage apex.

A tanker boom operator's view showing the air refuelling receptacle above and behind the F-117A pilot's head.

By any other criteria, the F-117A is a military disaster. It has an abysmal weapons load, is subsonic, has poor un-refuelled range, lacks radar and is a sitting duck in daylight. But low radar, infrared and sound signatures, plus the ability to operate while shielded by the cloak of night, more than compensated for what would ordinarily be shortcomings. It is an attack aircraft, intended to make a straight run to its target and to spend as little time in a defended area as possible.

The F-117A's main task is to mount pinpoint attacks by night against high-value, heavily defended targets. Its ability to avoid detection by radar enables it to penetrate deep into hostile territory. The impetus for the project was operational experience in the Vietnam War in the period 1965 to 1972, and the Middle East war of October 1973. In these conflicts, radar-guided surface-to-air missiles (SAMs) represented a threat to strike aircraft that could not be negated by tactics or countermeasures.

Two internal bays are mounted in the F-117A to carry its weapons – mainly laser-guided bombs. These are released in the general direction of the intended target and, in the final seconds before impact,

The F-117A's weapons are principally laser-guided bombs carried in two internal bays.

➤ *Forward and downward-looking infrared (FLIR/DLIR) and a Honeywell inertial navigation system provide navigation and targeting.*

Did you know?
Able to penetrate hostile airspace without being seen by radars or infrared sensors, the F-117 can then use its sophisticated target acquisition and designation system to score strikes against vital targets with pinpoint accuracy.

'I think the jet is now about as deadly and as capable as we have ever had it. Where we are today is probably the most lethal as far as our systems and the signature of the aircraft is concerned.'

Lt Col Todd Flesch.

the laser picks out the target, allowing the bombs to steer themselves to a direct hit. Each weapon's impact is recorded on an internal videotape system for real-time battle damage assessment. The planning system is designed to free the pilot from the task of getting to the target so he can devote all of his attention to the most important job: hitting the target with pin-point accuracy.

For stealth reasons the F-117A does not rely on radar for navigation or targeting. For navigation and weapon aiming, the aircraft is equipped with a forward-looking infrared (FLIR) and a downward-looking infrared (DLIR) with laser designator, supplied by Raytheon. The aircraft uses a Honeywell inertial navigation system and has multi-channel pitot static tubes installed in the nose. Multiple ports along the length of the tubes provide differential pressure readings; the flight control computers compare these in order to provide the aircraft's flight data.

Advanced F-117A designs were proposed for the US Navy after the aircraft's success in Operation *Desert Storm*. The F-117AN was followed by the afterburner-equipped, air-to-air capable A/F-117AX, both featuring a single-piece bubble canopy, folding wings and a conventional horizontal stabiliser. There were serious concerns over how well the delicate RAM would hold up under conditions at sea. Neither project came to fruition.

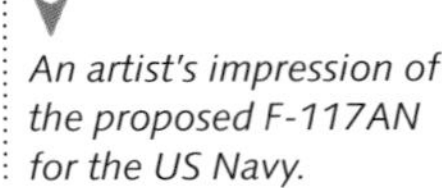

An artist's impression of the proposed F-117AN for the US Navy.

Did you know?

In the early 1990s, Lockheed tried to promote several naval versions of the F-117, with various designations such as the 'F-117N' and 'A/F-117X'. The designs showed modified wings and tail surfaces. The Navy was not interested.

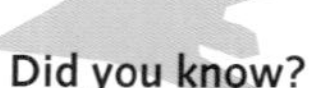

Did you know?

The F-117 has no gun, and is not capable of carrying external air-to-air missiles – but it could carry a wide range of air-to-ground ordnance internally.

The Nighthawk's bomb bays are located side-by-side with one-piece doors opening inwards from a hinge on the centreline. Each bay is 15ft 5in (4.7m) long and contains a retractable hoist, or trapeze, for stores carriage, which swings down and forward from the bomb bay. This is of inestimable value for groundcrews loading the weapons, allowing easy all-round access to the bomb carriage mechanism. Bay doors and weapon aiming are managed on a control panel immediately below the left-hand multi-function display. The weapons are released directly into the airstream from the hoists during an attack.

In order to knock out hardened targets, the F-117A relies on the deadly accuracy of the laser-guided bomb which currently offers the best way to achieve precision without causing extensive collateral

➤ *Two one-piece bomb-bay doors are hinged at the centreline.*

Two weapon loaders use an MHU-194/E Manually Operated Lift Truck (MOT) to load a GBU-27 laser-guided bomb.

A standard mechanised hoist is used for loading munitions onto the weapons bay trapeze.

Laser-guided bombs dropping from a 49th Fighter Wing F-117A .

'This is a strategic weapon that really reshaped how the USAF looked at strategic warfare. It doesn't matter what defences you put up, how deep you try to hide or how much you surround yourself with collateral damage, this airplane will come and get you.'

Lt Col Chris Knehans, commander of the 7th Fighter Squadron *Screaming Demons*.

damage. Therefore, the 2,000lb-class laser-guided bomb remains the F-117A's main weapon. Warhead options include the standard Mk84 high-explosive (GBU-10C/D/E/F and GBU-27, which is unique to the Nighthawk) and the BLU-109B low-level laser-guided penetration warhead, designed specifically with extreme accuracy for the F-117A, which, owing to its high cost, is used sparingly; Paveway II (GBU-10) and the more recent Paveway III (GBU-24/27/EGBU-27) guidance kit. Missiles carried can include Raytheon AGM-65 Maverick and Raytheon AGM-88 HARM anti-radar air-to-surface missiles.

The Paveway II computer control and guidance (CCG) unit uses full-deflection guidance, moving the front fins fully to alter the bomb's path. A third type of laser-guided bomb, the 500lb (227kg) GBU-12, which is a Mk82 bomb with Paveway II kits, has been used in special circumstances. It has known nuclear capability and consequently a nuclear strike role.

The F-117A is fully capable of level, loft, dive, dive toss and low-altitude drogue delivery (LADD) weapon release manoeuvres, but usually uses straight and level overfly delivery. A pair of co-ordinated infrared sensors, positioned to look forward (FLIR) and downward (DLIR), allow the pilot to 'acquire' a target in the dark of night. A laser, integral to each IR turret, can be directed onto a selected target providing a reference point for the guidance systems of the 'smart' bombs.

Aerodynamically, the F-117A is naturally unstable. It relies on the many vortices created by its sharp edges to form a lifting airflow pattern. The wing forms a simple aerofoil by having three flat sections above and two below. The flat under-wing surfaces blend into the under-fuselage surfaces to create a whole lifting surface below the aircraft. Contrary to some reports, the F-117A has more than adequate handling characteristics and considerable agility for an aircraft of its size and power.

On-board computers monitor the aircraft's orientation in the air and execute thousands of small electro-hydraulic adjustments that keep it flying smoothly.

The underside of the wing and fuselage blend to create a lifting surface.

F-117As have more agility, when lightly loaded, than their engine power suggests.

Did you know?

For the first few years of the programme pilots had no simulator. They trained on a no-motion, no-feedback cockpit procedure trainer (CPT) at Lockheed's Burbank facility.

Without flaps or afterburner the F-117A's take-off performance is laboured.

The 'fly-by-wire' flight control system, which has quadruple redundancy, was adapted from the F-16 Fighting Falcon. With neither flaps nor afterburner, the F-117A's take-off performance is ponderous, using up a lot of runway before reaching the type's 180kt unstick speed. The radio antenna is retracted when not required, since to extend it means a dramatic increase in RCS.

There is nothing special about the flight garments worn by the F-117A pilots. The pilot sits on a standard Boeing ACES II ejection seat and looks at conventional instruments and controls. The F-117A's cockpit layout is similar to other modern-day fighters, with the exception of a large video monitor in the centre to display infrared imagery from on-board sensors. The cockpit has a Kaiser Electronics head-up display (HUD) and a full-colour moving map. Highly accurate navigational positioning was also critical, and for this avionics role the 'Skunk Works' adapted an inertial navigation system (INS) developed for the B-52 Stratofortress. Two multi-

The pilot sits on a standard ACES II ejection seat. (Daniel J. March)

F-117A's cockpit layout is similar to that of other modern day fighters, with the exception of a video monitor to display infrared imagery from onboard sensors.

function display indicator units display a wide variety of imagery, mission data or diagnostic information.

The aircraft is flown with a central stick and the throttles are positioned on the left-hand console, while the right-hand console contains the pilot interface to the flight control and mission control computers. Once airborne, the pilot becomes little more than a systems monitor, usually leaving the actual flying to the sophisticated autopilot and auto-throttle. Challenges are posed by the F-117A, though – visibility from the faceted cockpit is poor and is believed to have contributed to accidents. F-117As tend to fly together in an echelon formation because of the limited visibility, rather than wingtip-to-wingtip as in, say, an F-16. The fact that the pilot must both fly and perform attacks by himself is another test of skill. The pilot must juggle multiple roles, allowing the autopilot system to direct him on his final attack run to the target while he releases the bomb and guides it to the target. Despite, or maybe because of, such

F-117As tend to fly together in echelon because of the limited lateral view from the cockpit.

challenges, one pilot called it 'a marvel to fly' and 'more cerebral' than other fighters. They often simulated bombing 'a guy's toolshed in his backyard, or something small, just for practice'.

The faceted shape imposes an estimated 20 per cent drag (and fuel consumption) penalty, and the heavily-shielded engine nozzles limit thrust and engine efficiency. On landing, the F-117A approaches the runway fast and flat, has a fairly fast touch-down speed and routinely uses a Pioneer Aerospace brake parachute, deploying this from between the fins as soon as the nosewheel touches the runway. The aircraft does have an arrester hook, but this is

The F-117A approaches the runway fast and flat for landing.

F-117As have no flaps so touchdown is fast. (Richard Cooper)

strictly for emergency use, since it has to be activated explosively.

Aerial refuelling is accomplished through a roll-over refuelling receptacle just aft of the canopy. A small rear-facing light is positioned to illuminate this receptacle. In a combat situation, this is the only light that is ever illuminated on an F-117A during the course of a darkened, radio-silent mission. Pilots describe the F-117A as pleasant and smooth to fly, if not entirely forgiving. Its characteristics are not unlike those of

With a high landing speed a brake parachute is essential to assist braking.

delta-wing aircraft, and the Nighthawk flies nose-high at low speeds and decelerates rapidly in a sharp turn. The thrust-to-weight ratio at maximum take-off weight is 0.4:1, which is not generous, especially in high temperature conditions. However,

'One of the great success stories of recent years. We simply could not have done what we've done as effectively and efficiently, and at as low a cost to life – both ours and the enemy's – if we hadn't had the stealth capability.'

Dick Cheney,
US Secretary of Defense.

the aircraft is surprisingly agile considering its size. Flight duty on the type has been regarded as an elite job, and pilots have tended to be very experienced in other types of combat aircraft. There is evidence that fatigue was chronic among early F-117A pilots, who flew only at night. At times, it caused pilots to become disorientated.

Did you know?

Many early F-117 pilots suffered considerable fatigue, and as a result of constantly flying at night put their mental time clocks out of sequence – and sometimes resulted in spatial disorientation.

Red marks show the location of the F-117's arrester hook.

JUST CAUSE

Thirteen months after the public announcement of its existence, the F-117A went into combat for the first time. Constant antagonism between the US and Panamanian dictator Gen Manuel Noriega had led US President George Bush to order that Noriega be removed from power by force. As diversions to ground operations, F-117As were assigned to perform pinpoint bombing strikes. The selection of the F-117A for the mission was based solely on its precision capability, not stealth, as the Panamanians had no real air defences. On the night of 20 December 1989, two aircraft from the 37th Tactical Fighter Wing initiated a co-ordinated air and ground attack against Gen Noriega's Panamanian Defence Force (PDF) base at Rio Hato, Panama, as part of Operation *Just Cause*. Each F-117A dropped a 2,000lb bomb adjacent to the Rio Hato barracks just before US 82nd Airborne troops attacked and overran the base with minimal casualties on either side. Two other Nighthawks were on hand to back up an attempt to capture General Noriega, and two more were deployed as spares.

The six aircraft departed Tonopah on the evening of 19 December 1989 and flew to Panama with the help of mid-air refuelling. The attempt to capture Noriega did not materialise, and in the end only the two aircraft assigned to the primary target actually performed strikes. There was some confusion at the last moment and the F-117As missed their aim points, although the results were as desired. In any case, US military forces proved well-organised and effective, and by the next day Panama was in US hands.

An F-117A receiving fuel from a KC-135Q Stratotanker.

DESERT SHIELD

Less than a month after delivery of the last F-117A, disturbing events began to unfold in the Middle East. On 2 August 1990, Saddam Hussein ordered three Iraqi Army divisions to invade neighbouring Kuwait. When diplomatic efforts failed to convince Iraq to withdraw, US President Bush responded to the request by Saudi Arabia's King Fahd to help protect his

Did you know?

The undeniable 'star' of the first Gulf War was the F-117A, which performed precision ground attacks against a number of targets. It led the fixed-wing aerial attack on the first night, hitting key defences and communication targets.

The partly underground hardened aircraft shelters at Khamis Mushayt accommodated the F-117A on a taxi-through basis. (Ian Macfadyen)

country. Saddam Hussein was getting into position to move into Saudi Arabia and assert control over the world's oil supplies. Operation *Desert Shield* was launched by the US on 7 August 1990.

As part of the massive build-up of air power, 20 F-117As left Tonopah early on 19 August 1990 bound for Langley AFB, Virginia, supported by KC-135Q tankers. They then flew direct to King Khalid Air Base at Khamis Mushait, Saudi Arabia (generally known as 'Tonopah East'), a high desert location situated at 6,800ft and bordered by mountains, with KC-10A Extenders in support. The transit flight involved 14–16 hours in the cockpit and four to six aerial refuellings.

Unlike most other US fighters, which were frequently operated from the flightline at their desert bases with only a roof to protect them from the scorching sunshine, the F-117As were assigned individual aircraft shelters offering them a shield from possible air attack. They were well out of range of Iraqi 'Scud' missiles and also safeguarded from the prying cameras of Soviet satellites.

In the meantime, the confrontation with the Iraqis settled into a sitting war, with both sides trading propaganda and jockeying for political position. On 12 January 1991, the US Congress voted to allow the use of force to remove the Iraqis from Kuwait, in support of a UN resolution demanding that Iraq pull out of the country. On 15 January, the deadline specified by the UN resolution expired.

'The F-117 allowed us to strike the "heart" of the enemy – downtown Baghdad – not only on Day 1, but night after night. Stealth allowed us to maintain continuous pressure on vital targets set, anywhere in Iraq.'

Lt Gen Charles A. Horner, commander of CENTAF, CENTCOM's air component.

DESERT STORM

On 16 January 1991, the F-117As were briefed for their strikes, as they were to be among the leading elements in the air war. Several in-flight refuellings were to be required for each mission. Their tasks included the elimination of air defence centres and other vital elements in the Iraqi war machine to allow conventional strike aircraft to make further raids unharmed. The Iraqi capital, Baghdad, was the prime target, defended by some 4,000 anti-aircraft guns and SAM launchers.

At 02.35hrs the following morning, Iraqi guns opened fire, despite the fact that the air attacks had not actually commenced. However, eight F-117As were moving into Iraqi airspace, together with F-15E Strike Eagles that were assigned to destroy 'Scud' missile launch sites in Iraq. At 02.51hrs,

Did you know?

In F-117 operations, a dozen aircraft could precisely deliver twenty-four 2,000lb laser-guided bombs on nearly as many separate targets, all without any dedicated support aircraft other than tankers.

Did you know?

During Operation *Desert Storm* F-117s were the only aircraft that attacked 'downtown' Baghdad targets, more heavily defended than any other Eastern European targets at the height of the Cold War. They did it with impunity.

one of the F-117As dropped a laser-guided bomb on a bunker that contained an air defence control centre. It blew off the bunker's doors.

The aimless firing overhead Baghdad went silent at 02.56hrs. There had been nothing to shoot at, although ironically the F-117As were just approaching the city, completely undetected. Moments later, they hit communications centres, including the Iraqi AF headquarters, an air defence centre, and one of Saddam Hussein's palaces.

The Baghdad air defences opened up again, while F-117As that still had bombs aboard went on to hit secondary objectives. Minutes later, a wave of Tomahawk cruise missiles began to hit leadership targets, such as the Iraqi Ba'ath Party headquarters, and shorted out power stations, which in turn knocked out the power grid.

At 03.30hrs, Iraqi air defences picked up a large attack force heading towards the capital. In reality, it was a fleet of decoy drones, backed up by conventional strike aircraft carrying high-speed anti-radiation missiles (HARMs). As the air defence radars locked onto the drones, the HARMs knocked out the radars.

A second wave of F-117As hit Baghdad at 04.00hrs. Approach to the city was a fear-some experience. From 150km away, one pilot described it as looking like 'a charcoal grill on the fourth of July', glowing with the fire of massed anti-aircraft guns. The Iraqis had poured anti-aircraft fire into the night sky over Baghdad, almost at random and without effect. One F-117A pilot simply lowered his seat so he could not be distracted by the 'fireworks', thereby allowing him to concentrate on his target run. The F-117As

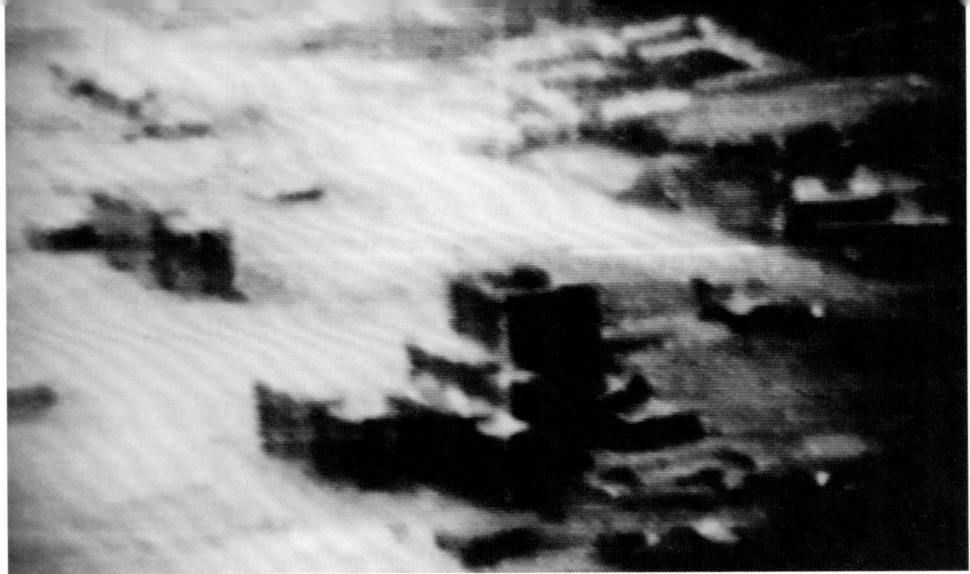

A still photo from an F-117A's DLIR turret, with the 'cross-hairs' firmly assigned over a communications centre in downtown Baghdad. (via Brian Strickland)

hit some of the same targets that had been bombed in the first wave, as well as air bases and command and control sites all over Iraq. These two waves dropped thirty-three laser-guided bombs (LGBs) and scored twenty-three hits.

'The F-117 allowed us to do things we would only have dreamed of in past conflicts. The F-117 was the premier star of the air campaign.'

Lt Gen Charles A. Horner, the air component commander under General Norman Schwarzkopf.

Did you know?

Striking targets in Baghdad in 1991 meant attacking one of the world's most heavily defended cities. Due to its stealth attributes and consequent ability to avoid detection, the F-117 was the only aircraft to go there.

A third and final wave came in just before dawn to hit chemical and biological weapons bunkers. It was considered that sunlight would help kill any anthrax spores scattered from the bio-weapons sites. Unfortunately cloudy weather made targeting difficult, and of sixteen LGBs dropped, only five scored hits.

The F-117As returned to their Saudi Arabian base, their pilots exhausted and glad to be alive. Much to their surprise, all of them got back safely. Despite substantial worries, stealth had worked. Actually the F-117As had attacked one of the most heavily-defended targets anywhere with complete impunity.

➤ *A pilot's view of a hardened aircraft shelter recorded by the IRADS onboard his aircraft.* (via Brian Strickland)

'The skies of Baghdad were lit up like Las Vegas – but they did not have a clue where we were coming from.'

Lt Col Ralph Gerchell, who led the first wave of Nighthawks into Baghdad. He coined a name for the 37th TFW – 'Team Stealth'.

A daylight attempt to hit Baghdad with conventional aircraft on 19 January failed, causing little damage to the target and the loss of two F-16s. Consequently, from that point on, only F-117As and/or Tomahawk cruise missiles were used to attack the city. The F-117As continued the assaults on command and control centres, chemical/biological weapons dumps, and other targets. On 21 January, they hit and crippled a nuclear research facility in Baghdad, putting it out of operation. Throughout all the missions, the Iraqis did not know an F-117A attack was in progress until the bombs actually detonated.

The F-117As followed up F-111 daylight raids on Iraqi AF hardened aircraft shelters. The strikes had been made with conventional bombs, which had failed to dent the shelters. Iraq began to hide more of its military aircraft away in the shelters. The USAF realised its error and rearmed the F-117As with hardened penetration bombs, as intelligence indicated that some of the Iraqi aircraft were being loaded for a chemical attack.

On the night of 24 January, the F-117As struck the shelters again, scoring twenty

▲ *Subsequent reconnaissance photos showing the aftermath of a direct hit by a laser-guided bomb.*

hits that punched into the shelters and blasted them out. Two days later, the Iraqi AF began to flee to Iran, where its aircraft were interned and repainted with Iranian markings. Therefore, F-117A strikes on the shelters were stepped up to destroy as many Iraqi aircraft as possible before they could fly out of reach.

By 27 January, General Norman Schwarzkopf, head of Coalition forces, had moved most of the air assets from attacks against Iraq to strikes on Iraqi forces in Kuwait. Only the F-117As and F-111s continued attacks on Iraq itself. On 5 February, the F-111s were moved to attacks on Kuwait, leaving Iraq to the F-117As. Over the following weeks, the F-117As continued their strikes, while the Iraqis poured anti-aircraft fire into the sky in a vain hope of hitting one of them. They never scratched them, justifying the nickname the Saudis had given the aircraft: 'Shaba', Arabic for 'ghost'.

' I reached my aiming point, illuminating my target with my laser designator – we don't talk a lot about the details of that – and went down in a dive, looking up into the crosshairs of my display. I successfully dropped a laser-guided bomb (GBU-27) on the specialised target and banked to get out of there post-haste.'

Maj Mike Mahor, pilot of an F-117 in the second assault on Baghdad in 1991.

The F-117As were kept busy hitting Iraqi chemical, biological and nuclear warfare centres in the rest of the country. Bad weather dogged the strikes, reducing visibility and bombing effectiveness, although when the skies were clear the

F-117A #832 outside its shelter at Khamis Mushayt with 24 mission markings painted below the cockpit.

results of the attacks were devastating. The aircraft were also assigned to other well-defended targets as opportunities arose.

It was not until the night of 27 February 1991 that the F-117As returned to Baghdad, going 'downtown' with two waves of

➤ *Most of the F-117As carried 'theatre art' on the inside of the nose wheel and bomb doors. Spell Bound was painted on #797.* (Ian Macfadyen)

strikes that did particular damage to the Ba'ath Party headquarters. A third wave was called off, and a short time later a ceasefire was announced. The Gulf War was over.

Many of the *Desert Storm* attack videos that were shown on news bulletins around the world came from F-117A DLIR sensors. The precision of the attacks, with some bombs being guided down ventilation shafts into the heart of communications bunkers, did much to convince public opinion that there was no indiscriminate bombing of civilian targets.

During the Gulf War, 45 F-117As and some 60 pilots flew a total of 1,271 combat sorties, dropped 2,030 tons of bombs, flew over 6,900 hours and demonstrated accuracy unmatched in the history of air warfare. Although only 36 F-117As were deployed in *Desert Storm*, accounting for 2.5 per cent of the total force of 1,900 fighters and bombers, they flew more than a third of the bombing runs on the first day of the war. Although more than 3,000 anti-aircraft guns and 60 surface-to-air missile batteries protected Baghdad, the 'Black Jets' of the 37th TFW owned the skies over the city and, for that matter, the country.

➤➤ *En route back to Tonopah this 37TFW F-117A appeared in public for the first time outside the USA at the Paris Air Show in June 1991.* (Andrew P. March)

TR
37 TFW
VFA-137
100

The first public visit by an F-117A to the UK was made by #830 when it attended the RAF Mildenhall Air Fete in May 1992.

The F-117As began to return to Tonopah on 1 April 1991, although a detachment remained at 'Tonopah East' after the Gulf War to help enforce sanctions against Iraq. After numerous violations of the ceasefire agreement, on 13 January 1993, six 37th TFW aircraft performed strikes on air defence targets in southern Iraq. Results were mixed, due to bad weather, but overall the missions achieved their goals.

'Stealth technology saved lives. It saved not only our lives, as pilots, but also shortened the war due to our ability to destroy targets at a quicker speed. If we didn't have Stealth technology, it would have been a totally different war.'

Capt Wesley Cockman, USAF F-117 pilot on return from the first Gulf War.

An announcement in January 1990 revealed that the F-117A force would be moving from Tonopah to Holloman AFB, New Mexico, in 1992. The transfer required the setting-up of new facilities at Holloman, including a RAM spray unit. Renumbered the 49th Fighter Wing, the aircraft and crews completed the move between May and July 1992. The personnel were no longer separated from their families, nor shuttled to and from Tonopah by air.

The three old squadrons of the 37th TFW were re-numbered as the 7th, 8th and 9th Fighter Squadrons in mid-1993. The 8th

Did you know?
In the 1990s, Lockheed revived earlier plans to sell new-build F-117s to Britain, but the RAF had no politically justifiable formal need and little money to spend as its budget was largely committed to the Eurofighter Typhoon.

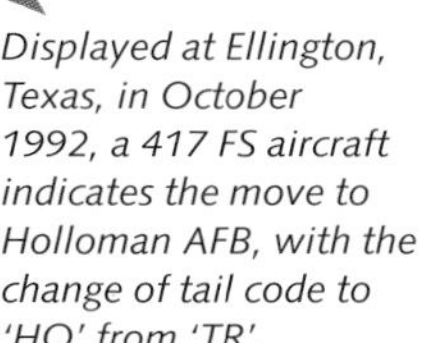

Displayed at Ellington, Texas, in October 1992, a 417 FS aircraft indicates the move to Holloman AFB, with the change of tail code to 'HO' from 'TR'.

An F-117A taxies in towards the extensive new hangar facilities at Holloman AFB. (Daniel J. March)

F-117A #809 shows its assignment to the 9th FS 'Flying Knights' of the 49th FW at Holloman. (Daniel J. March)

The 49th FW commander's aircraft with the badges of the 7th, 8th and 9th Fighter Squadrons on the fin top (Daniel J. March)

and 9th were the operational units with an authorised strength of 18 aircraft each, the 7th being a training squadron, named the 'Screamin Demons', which served as the transition training unit. It prepared experienced USAF pilots (and some from other air arms, including Royal Air Force exchange officers) for assignment to the Nighthawk, this name being given to the aircraft in June 1994.

Pre-flight operations at Holloman where F-117A #802 is being refuelled from an underground fuel system in its hangar.

Did you know?
For the first seven years of its operational career, the F-117 was flown almost exclusively at night to protect the secrets of its revolutionary shape.

Originally, the 4450th Tactical Group, based at Tonopah, operated A-7D Corsair IIs for training F-117A pilots. The A-7D, being of similar size and having comparable flying characteristics to the F-117A, proved useful in training the original cadre of F-117A fliers, as well as providing the unit with a useful 'cover' for its operational role. However, with much of the secrecy lifted, the A-7, proving expensive to operate as all other front-line USAF units had retired the type by this time, was deemed surplus to requirements and the two-seat Northrop T-38 Talon took on the role. Although a two-

A T-38 Talon used for pilot training by the 49th FW.

7th FS F-117A on a training sortie over typical New Mexico desert topography.

seat F-117A was studied and contemplated for production, only the operational single-seat F-117A was ever procured.

Stepping into such a high-tech and expensive warplane, with no dual-seat trainer in which to familiarise, was a daunting prospect. Much time was spent flying practice sorties in the T-38 and, more relevantly, hours of simulator time

Did you know?

Because of security concerns in the mid-1980s, there were no patches that showed the F-117, said 'F-117', or the name 'Nighthawk'. All patches that related to the F-117 programme had obscure symbols and animals on them, and even these came under security restrictions (scorpions, dragons, etc). One patch showed a goat being chased by an A-7 aircraft with the words 'Goatsuckers'. This patch was presumably worn by A-7 pilots (possibly instructor pilots) who chased the F-117 during training missions.

➤
F-117A turns on to finals to land at Holloman at the end of a training flight. (Jamie Hunter)

were required before an F-117A pilot made his first solo – officially becoming a 'Bandit'. Bandit numbers were awarded from the earliest days of the *Senior Trend* programme as a secret identity for each pilot that has flown the F-117A. In the 1980s, the pilot was not even allowed to tell his own family of his 'Bandit' number, such was the security surrounding the aircraft and its operations.

Pilot training at Holloman was undertaken by the 7th FS, later re-designated as the 7th Combat Training Squadron (CTS), known as the 'Bunyaps'. The unit's primary mission was to train all prospective F-117A pilots for the complex night formation or single-ship

Formation of Holloman-based F-117A Nighthawk, F-4 Phantom and T-38 Talon. (Jamie Hunter)

missions that the operational squadrons are expected to perform, including acquiring targets and delivering weapons. The instructors on the two-seat T-38 Talons were all experienced F-117A 'Bandits' and frequently augmented the operational F-117A squadrons during peacetime and combat deployments.

The training course lasted three months and was extremely intensive, the pilot having to complete the tough flying syllabus successfully and master hours of academic and simulator training programmes. After completing the training, 'new' pilots went to one of the 49th FW's two operational F-117A squadrons.

The tactics employed by the operational F-117A squadrons are necessarily closely guarded: 'We don't talk too much about how we do our business, tactics are like a game of chess and displaying your moves to potential enemies is obviously undesirable,' said one. What is known is that the Nighthawk is designed to destroy important heavily defended targets particularly at the start of a campaign. 'Decapitation' of the enemy's leadership and destruction of its command and control facilities can throw hostile forces into disarray. Penetrating at night, attacks are most usually planned as two- or four-ships and are conducted with split-second timing and accuracy. The advanced avionics and autopilot allow F-117A crews to receive targeting information to a precise grid reference at short notice and be airborne to deliver their munitions with minimal delay. Despite the aircraft's 'stealth' characteristics, the F-117s have often operated as part of a package including ECM aircraft (usually US Navy or Marine Corps EA-6B Prowlers) and HARM anti-radiation missile-equipped fighters, along with tanker support where necessary.

The F-117A has also helped give the USAF the ability to project its power with

A Nighthawk of the 9th FS that made the long Pacific crossing to South Korea.

speed and over great distances. As the 49th FW, with a cadre of aircraft and aircrew mainly drawn from the 8th FS, was preparing for combat in Operation *Iraqi Freedom* in early 2003, the 9th FS was deployed to South Korea. With anxiety rising concerning the attempts by North Korea to assemble a nuclear arsenal and the relationship between that country and the US worsening, the presence of the Nighthawks would represent a powerful deterrent to North Korea's ambitions. Initially intended as a short-term deployment, the 9th FS remained in Korea long after the 8th FS had returned from the Gulf.

The transit flights were particularly memorable. As an F-117A pilot recalled: 'We deployed to Hawaii and then on to South Korea as part of a multiple tanker set-up with six F-117As, crossing the Pacific. The rendezvous with tankers that have launched from afar, to meet us over the middle of an ocean, was particularly impressive. The many rendezvous all worked perfectly and I'm thinking this is just amazing. I've just been in charge of a flight of multiple KC-135s and two F-117As transiting the Pacific Ocean. The F-117A with its autopilot and cockpit comfort helps make this "global reach" possible.'

'We treat the pilots like bats. They come here Monday afternoons and they don't see daylight until next Friday. They won't sleep if they see that sun. It's like a vampire's convention.'

Anon.

Did you know?

The Lockheed 'Skunk Works' consistently delivered F-117s on time and within budget. For the fifty-nine operational aircraft delivered, the unit cost averaged $42.6 million, roughly comparable to the flyaway cost of other existing twin-engined fighters.

Three F-117As line up behind a tanker while preparing for deployment to Aviano, Italy, in 1999.

Did you know?

In Saudi Arabia, the name used as a call-sign was Shabah (or Shaba) since it was close to the Arabic word for ghost, and that was what the local people called it. During *Allied Force* (1999) the 'shabah' call-sign was heard for training flights.

The conflict in the Balkans, following the break-up of Yugoslavia, had been ongoing since the early 1990s. The largest-scale military action involving multi-national assets in coalition took place in early 1999, in an effort to halt the policies of violence and repression directed at the majority Albanian population in Kosovo on the part of Yugoslav President Slobodan Milosevic and his regime. On 21 February 1999, a dozen F-117As arrived at Aviano Air Base in Italy as part of the NATO military build-up for possible combat operations. As the 8th Expeditionary Fighter Squadron, they formed part of the USAF's 31st Air Expeditionary Wing.

In the opening phase of *Allied Force*, aimed primarily at Yugoslavia's integrated air defence system, NATO air forces conducted more than 400 sorties. During

Arriving at Aviano on 22 February 1999, one of twelve F-117As of the 9th Expeditionary Fighter Squadron.

One of the twenty-five Nighthawks eventually based at Spangdahlen, Germany, with the 52nd Air Expeditionary Wing.

the first two nights (24–25 March 1999), F-117As from the 8th Expeditionary Fighter Squadron participated in air strikes against targets in the Balkans during NATO operations. Often they operated as part of strike packages alongside the USAF's other 'stealth' asset, the B-2 Spirit. Other targets that were subsequently hit included Serbia's power grid, for which the specially-developed BLU-114/B weapon was used for the first time by F-117As on 2 May. A total of twenty-five Nighthawks were involved, the original deployment of twelve jets later being augmented by thirteen more, comprising a dozen to form a second Expeditionary Fighter Squadron (the 9th EFS) and one more to replace that shot down by a Serbian SAM battery on 27 March. The 9th EFS complement of Nighthawks arrived at their operating base, Spangdahlem in Germany, on 4 April. Towards the end of May, all F-117A operations as part of *Allied Force* were concentrated at Spangdahlem. They continued to fly sorties, mainly to targets in Serbia where air defences made it harder for non-stealthy aircraft to get through safely, until NATO halted combat operations on 10 June.

Once again, the Nighthawk force had proved itself in combat, despite the loss of one of its aircraft. The 49th FW's jets started arriving back at Holloman on 26 June, having notched up over 1,000 sorties. However, *Allied Force* taught the USAF some lessons about the F-117A, among them the need to improve its all-weather capability as around half of all Nighthawk missions during the conflict had to be cancelled for weather-related reasons.

'We had the capability on board to guide a bomb via laser to the target, but now, within the last few months, we also have JDAM integration that brings an all-weather precision strike capability that we haven't had before.'

Lt Col Todd Flesch, Director of Operations with the 8th Fighter Squadron
The Black Sheep.

➤
Wreckage of F-117A 82-0806 that was brought down by Serbian/Yugoslav air defences on 22 March 1999.

One F-117A has been lost in combat. On 27 March 1999, during the Kosovo war, the Serbian/Yugoslav air defence 3rd Battalion of the 259th Missile Brigade, equipped with the Isayev S-125 'Neva-M' (NATO designation SA-3 'Goa'), shot down F-117A 82-0806. According to US Gen Wesley Clark and other NATO commanders, Yugoslav air defences found that they could detect F-117As with their 'obsolete' Soviet radars operating on long wavelengths. This, combined with the loss of stealth when the jets got wet or opened their bomb bays, made them visible on radar screens. The pilot survived and was quickly rescued by NATO forces. The wreckage of the Nighthawk was not promptly destroyed by bombing and the Serbs are believed to have invited Russian personnel to inspect the remains, inevitably compromising the US stealth technology. The SAMs were most likely guided manually with the help of thermal imagers and laser range-finders. Reportedly, several SA-3s were launched,

one of which probably exploded close enough to the F-117A to force the pilot to eject.

The first F-117A loss occurred on 20 April 1982 when the first production aircraft crashed on its maiden flight. Two further examples were subsequently lost during service with the 4450th Tactical Group. Some years after the type was revealed, an F-117A crashed during a night training exercise into the Zuni Tribal Reservation in New Mexico on 5 April 1995 and the pilot was killed. Another F-117A broke up during its final pass, while preparing to return to its base, at an airshow at the Glenn Martin State Airport near Baltimore, Maryland, on 14 September 1997, with the pilot ejecting safely. The crash was partly caught on video and occurred during a series of other accidents involving USAF aircraft, giving it a high profile. The fifty-three surviving jets were grounded while the problem was investigated. It turned out to be due to the failure of a control surface.

The wreckage of the downed Nighthawk came under close scrutiny, not least by Russian personnel eager to learn more about US stealth technology.

F-117As deployed to the Gulf several times during the late 1990s to support efforts to deprive Iraqi President Saddam Hussein of his Weapons of Mass Destruction (WMD) programmes and to force his compliance with the United Nations monitoring regime. These were carried out from 1996–98 under the auspices of Operation *Southern Watch*. Following President George W. Bush's declaration that Iraq was part of a so-called 'axis of evil' in the aftermath of the 11 September

➤
Three F-117As about to taxi for take-off at Al Jaber Air Base, Kuwait in support of Operation Southern Watch in March 1998.

➤➤
A pair of Nighthawks about to depart on a mission over Iraq at dusk during Southern Watch.

2001 terrorist attacks and the start of the 'Global War on Terrorism', this issue again came to a head at the beginning of 2003, when another vast military build-up in the Middle East prepared for the US-led war against Iraq that ultimately deposed Saddam Hussein from power. Twelve F-117As were deployed from Holloman

➤ *An F-117A assigned to the 8th Fighter Squadron receiving a final check on runway at Ahmed Al Jaber AB.*

An F-117A moves in to refuel from a KC-135 while an F-15E and F-16CJ wait their turn.

to Al Udeid in Qatar during February, where they formed part of the 379th Air Expeditionary Wing.

When the controversial Operation *Iraqi Freedom* was launched on the early morning of 20 March 2003, after the Iraqi regime failed to back down, Nighthawks were again chosen to lead the first night's air attacks, mounting so-called 'decapitation strikes' against key targets. Two aircraft were involved in an attack on that first night aimed at hitting

A group of coalition aircraft formate with a KC-135 while refuelling an F-15E Strike Eagle over Iraq during Operation Iraqi Freedom *in April 2003.*

a large bunker on the outskirts of Baghdad that was believed to house elements of the Iraqi political and military leadership, including Saddam Hussein. This mission was notable in that the weapon being used by the F-117As was the new EGBU-27 precision guided bomb, making its combat debut. Certification allowing F-117As to drop two of these weapons simultaneously had only been given a few hours before.

This Nighthawk indicates it has completed sixteen *Iraqi Freedom* missions with symbols below its cockpit.

As expected, the attack caught the Iraqi air defences completely off guard, and even though Saddam Hussein himself was not killed in the strike, it was an important early success for the Coalition. It also proved the effectiveness of the GPS-guided EGBU-27, which became the 'weapon of choice' for the F-117A in *Iraqi Freedom* as the 49th FW aircraft undertook further strikes against such targets as Iraq's military

Flying from Al Udeid AB in Qatar, this F-117A moves in towards a refuelling tanker during a mission over Iraq.

communications facilities and command bunkers.

The USAF says that F-117As flew more than eighty operational sorties during *Iraqi Freedom*, which ended on 14 April 2003, and that the type achieved an 89.3 per cent mission capable rate.

'Bats occasionally worked their way into F-117 hangars in Saudi Arabia. One night, a hungry bat turned right into an F-117 rudder and fell stunned to the floor. He flew away groggily, leaving behind a heightened impression of the aircraft's stealth. "I don't know what the radar return is for the vertical tails of the F-117 but I always thought it had to be more than an insect's," the reader said. "I guess I was wrong. There may be some 'science' in this – the ultrasound wavelengths used by bats are roughly the same as X-band radar."'

Aviation Week and Space Technology, 17 October 1991.

More than 100 different Operational Test and Evaluation (OT&E) projects have been carried out in relation to the F-117A during its lifetime of operational service, with Detachment 1 of the 53rd Test and Evaluation Group, a tenant unit at Holloman AFB since the Nighthawk fleet moved there, having been responsible. This unit is better known as the 'Dragon Test Team' after test pilot Pete Barnes had a green dragon like the invisible creature in the film *Pete's Dragon* painted on the F-117A in which he was about to make his first flight in 1982. Detachment 1 pioneered a new style of testing for the USAF, in which it was involved in the entire process of taking developments by Lockheed Martin from their inception to implementation on the front line, thus combining Developmental Test and Operational Test functions.

The unit has been unique in operating the only two F-117As to have dispensed with the standard black livery since the very early days of flight trials of the prototypes. In December 2003, its Nighthawk was unveiled in a two-tone grey livery,

In mid-1993, some ten years after the F-117A fleet was painted black, the third aircraft #782 acquired a light-blue overall paint scheme for daylight visibility testing. It was known as the 'Gray Ghost'.

Did you know?

Lockheed suggested an 'F-117B' to the USAF with more powerful engines to increase its range and payload, allowing it to carry over eight tonnes (18,000lb) of bombs, four internally, four externally. The external weapons were to be covered with RAM to keep the aircraft stealthy. Military budgets were tight and it was not pursued.

➤➤ *F-117A #835 was repainted in a two-tone grey scheme in December 2003 at Holloman AFB where it conducted visibility trials dubbed the 'Gray Dragon'.*

becoming known as the 'Gray Dragon'. The 'Dragon Test Team' was about to undertake a programme entitled F-117A Mission Effectiveness – Force Development Evaluation (FDE), which, among other things, looked into improving the survivability of the Nighthawk in daylight and developing tactics for such operations, something which had been under consideration for some years. A second 'Gray Dragon', this time in a single-tone scheme darker than that of the previous grey aircraft, took to the air in January 2006. It again embarked on tactical development, notably looking at how to employ the F-117A in conjunction with the F-22A Raptor, but the testing was cancelled before completion.

Over the last fifteen years, the F-117A fleet has undergone a continuous programme of upgrades at a cost of over $1,400m. Cockpit displays and navigation systems have been enhanced, with the aircraft now having a four-dimensional flight management system, which navigates to a designated coordinate at a specified time within one second. New instruments have been added, including a full-colour multi-functional display and digital moving map.

In 2000, Lockheed Martin began a Single Configuration Fleet (SCF) effort to modify the surviving F-117As to a consistent and up-to-date RAM configuration, the

REMOVE BEFORE FLIGHT
BEFORE FLIGHT
835

intention being to reduce maintenance time by 30 per cent and expenditure of RAM consumables by 20 per cent. A robotic system was used to apply a new RAM coating to fifty-one aircraft modified by 2005. The Block 2 upgrade allowed the F-117A to carry newer munitions, particularly the EGBU-27 900kg (2,000lb)

➤ *A GBU-27A Paveway III laser-guided bomb on a test drop from F-117 #784.*

bomb, an enhanced version of the GBU-27 that added GPS/INS guidance to the existing laser guidance system.

The 'Dragon Test Team' continued to test and help develop F-117A upgrades up until its disbandment on 1 October 2006 as part of the fleet's draw-down. During September 2003, time-sensitive targeting was demonstrated when a Detachment 1 Nighthawk sent images of a trials attack directly to the ground from the aircraft's cockpit. There was also a need to enhance the type's capability to carry 'smart' weapons, which first came to light as a result of its limitations in adverse weather conditions as demonstrated during *Allied Force*. The GBU-27 and EGBU-27 weapons were unique to the F-117A, not an ideal situation. Greater weapons commonality with other platforms was required, and the 'Dragon Test Team' was responsible for bringing about the integration of the Joint Direct Attack Munition (JDAM) into the Nighthawk fleet. The Wind-Corrected Munitions Dispenser (WCMD) and Small Diameter Bomb (SDB) were due to follow, enabling the F-117A to strike even more targets on a single mission, but both were cancelled when the aircraft's impending retirement was announced.

'The F-117, an aircraft whose history already contains as many secrets as it does legends.'
Lt Col Chris Knehans.

No other aircraft will be able to usurp the F-117A's place in history books as the first to employ stealth technology and the first to prove the concept in war. For a long time, it seemed the stuff of science fiction. It could fly across enemy skies and through the world's most advanced radar systems without being detected. This capability allowed the aircraft to perform reconnaissance missions and bomb critical

➤
A pair of F-117As escorting a B-2 Spirit stealth bomber. The aircraft are a generation apart in stealth technology development.

➤➤
An F-117A poses next to an early F-22 Raptor on the ramp at Edwards AFB in October 1999.

ED
ED

➤
The Raptor is very different from the Nighthawk's shape and performance.

targets, all without the enemy knowing who or what had hit them.

However, the Nighthawk is still very much an aircraft designed with technologies that were state-of-the-art in the late 1970s and early 1980s. Most noticeably its stealth technology and faceting, while still more advanced than that of any other aircraft except the B-2 Spirit and F-22A Raptor, is maintenance-intensive. Furthermore, the faceting technology represents an old counter-radar technique that has since been greatly refined. The technology that once made it a unique weapon system has now caught up with it, and the arrival of the stealthy F-22 in particular, with its air-to-ground capability, has led to its impending retirement. Even so, as described, 2004 and 2005 saw several mid-life improvement programmes being implemented on the F-117A, including an avionics upgrade, with others in progress up until the disbandment of the 'Dragon Test Team' which did so much to enhance the Nighthawk's effectiveness as a weapon system.

The increase of production of the F-22A, and its entry as an operational aircraft into the USAF, created much debate about retiring the F-117A fleet. Proponents of retiring the Nighthawk, who eventually won the day, have argued that high maintenance costs and older stealth technology that is vulnerable to long-wave radar, combined with a subsonic top speed, makes the F-117A more dangerous to fly. They contend that the Raptor is the logical successor, especially as it can fly at supersonic speeds without using afterburners, and thus can reach targets more quickly. The new 250lb small diameter bomb (SDB) now entering service, designed specifically to fit in the F-22A's internal munitions bays, has the same penetrating power as the larger 2,000lb BLU-109 bomb.

The draw-down of the F-117A has already quietly begun. The F-117A Weapons School deactivated, followed closely by the inactivation of the 53rd

A flypast of 25 F-117As over Holloman in October 2006 to mark the impending drawdown of the type. (Richard Cooper)

➤➤

An impressive line-up of Nighthawks at Holloman before the October 2006 flypast. (Richard Cooper)

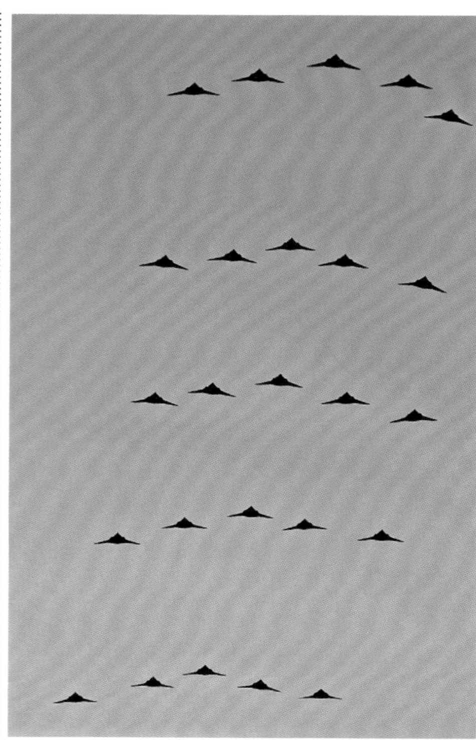

Test & Evaluation Group's Detachment 1, the famous 'Dragon Test Team', on 1 October 2006. The next unit to go was the 7th Fighter Squadron, the 'Screamin Demons', the F-117A's Formal Training Unit (FTU) which was disbanded on 15 December 2006. The FTU was de-activated because its mission was complete. There were enough qualified and experienced F-117A pilots to fly the Nighthawks until their retirement. Its final class ended with the graduation of five new Nighthawk pilots and the requalification of one more on 13 October 2006. Col David Goldfein, the 49th FW's commander, had the honour of receiving the last 'Bandit' number, 708. The 8th FS took over the 49th FW's T-38 Talon operations at Holloman, these aircraft now being used as chase and flight evaluation platforms.

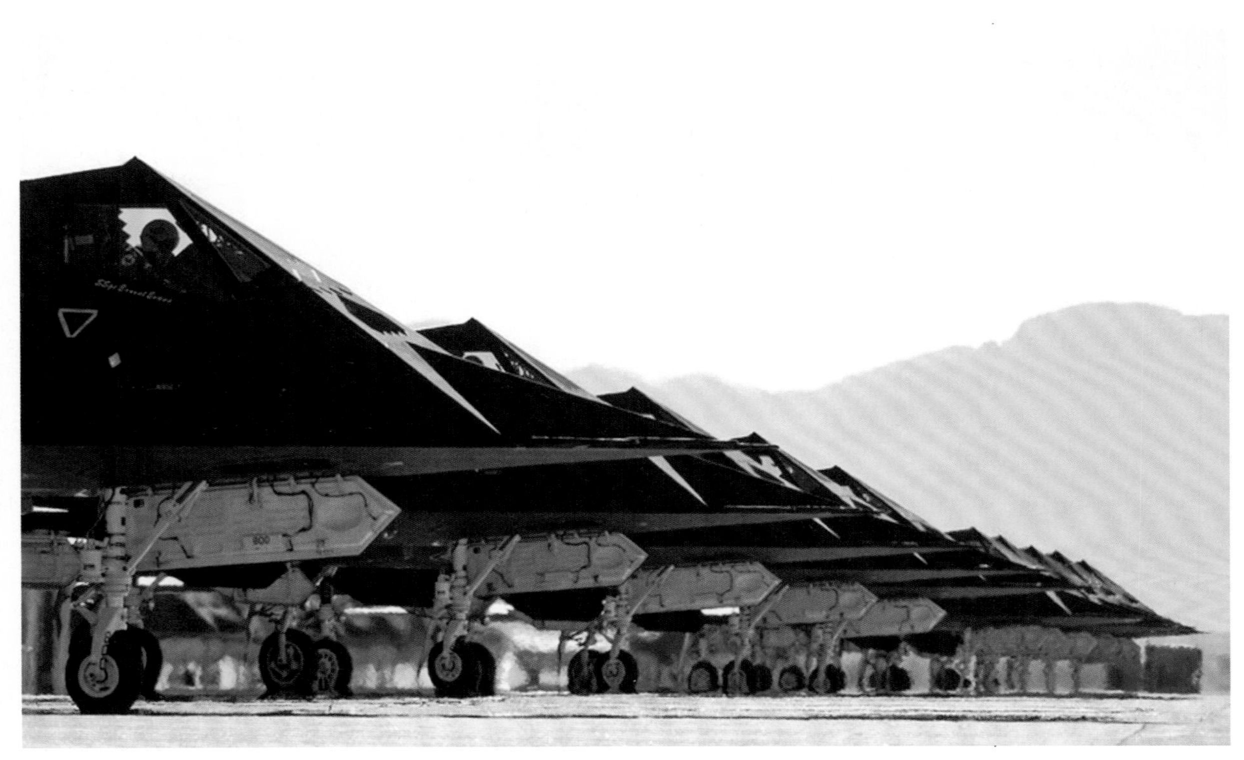

➤
The F-117As taxi to the runway at Holloman.
(Richard Cooper)

'The F-117, like all aircraft throughout our history, has a life cycle. It just gets old and becomes more expensive to operate. The F-22 will do "the future jobs that we have been called upon to do". The Raptor will allow quicker planning and execution of missions. It is a Grand Canyon leap ahead.'

Brig Gen David L. Goldfein, Holloman base commander.

Visiting the Royal International Air Tattoo at RAF Fairford in July 2003, a 49th FW F-117A made a spectacular flypast with the RAF's Red Arrows team.

USAF

The first ten F-117As were officially withdrawn on 31 December 2006, to make way for the incoming F-22A Raptors. Of the ten, four F-117As were kept in reserve at Holloman and six were flown to Tonopah on 12 March 2007 where their wings were removed and the aircraft stored in their original hangars. The remaining forty Nighthawks are due to be retired by October 2008. A few test aircraft at Edwards AFB and Palmdale will also be retired in 2008, which will account for the entire Nighthawk fleet. A pair of F-117As made a final visit to the UK to take part in the 60th anniversary of the US Air Force at the Royal International Air Tattoo at RAF Fairford in July 2007.

New F-22A Raptors are due to begin arriving at Holloman AFB direct from the production line between September and December 2008. By mid-2007, Congress had ordered 183 Raptors, and 36 have so far been earmarked for Holloman. The base's workforce of 2,000 people will remain. Should more F-22s be allocated, the 49th Fighter Wing will reactivate the 7th Fighter Squadron and host three squadrons rather than the two currently planned. The F-117A and the F-22 are the same size, so they can use the same hangars.

At least three complete F-117As are on display in the USA. The first aircraft to fly 79-10780 (FSD-1) is a gate guardian at Nellis AFB, and the second aircraft 79-10781 (FSD-2) is at the National Museum of the USAF at Wright-Patterson AFB in Ohio. The gate guardian at the Lockheed Martin Skunk Works at Palmdale is a composite comprising the remains of 79-10785 that crashed on 20 April 1982

FSD-1 #780, the first F-117 to fly, is preserved at Nellis AFB, Nevada.

on its first flight and parts from static test airframes 778 and 779. It is anticipated that further F-117As will go on display at selected museums after the aircraft are finally retired from service and their 'secrets' removed.

With just over a century of powered flight behind us, there are perhaps just a handful of aircraft that have stood out as true breakthroughs in technology. The F-117A Nighthawk is surely a candidate for this accolade, alongside legendary names such as the Wright 'Flyer', the Bell X-1 and Concorde, for pushing the boundaries of aviation technology to new levels. The stealth technology, which includes unique geometry and surface coatings, is still considered classified and sensitive.

The deserts of the western states of America have seen some unique sights over the years. Unimaginable designs have emerged, with some entering front-line service, a few confined to one-off concepts, while others . . . well, we will probably never know. But we do know about the F-117A, which still offers an awesome, dependable and vital capability. This is even more impressive given that its concept was conceived more than thirty years ago.

The second F-117 to fly, #781, is on display at the National Museum of the US Air Force at Wright Patterson AFB, Ohio.

'With the launch of these great aircraft today, the circle comes to a close – their service to our nation's defence fulfilled, their mission accomplished and a job well done. We send them today to their final resting place – a home they are intimately familiar with – their first and only home, outside of Holloman.'

Brig Gen David L. Goldfein. Holloman base commander, speaking on 12 March 2007 at the ceremony to mark the last flight of the first six F-117As to be retired.

LOCKHEED F-117A NIGHTHAWK

Span: 43ft 4in (13.20m)

Length: 65ft 11in (20.08m)

Height: 12ft 5in (3.78m)

Wing area: 1,140sq ft (105.9m2)

Service ceiling: 38,000ft (11,765m)

Mission range (without refuelling): Combat radius of 690 miles (1,112km)

Maximum speed: 646mph (1,040km/h). Marginally supersonic in a shallow dive

Cruising speed: 562mph (904km/h)

Maximum weight: 52,390lb (23,810kg)

Crew: Pilot only

Armament: Maximum weapons load 5,000lb (2,268kg): GBU-10 or GBU-27 Paveway LGBs carried in internal weapons bay, plus conventional bombs up to 2,000lb (907kg) weight each, typically GBU-10 and GBU-27, up to a maximum load of 5,000lb (2,268kg). Tactical munitions dispensers and infrared and laser-guided missiles, AGM-65 Maverick or HARM can also be carried. New weapons include GBU-30s (JDAM) and JSOW.

Engines: Two 10,800lb st (48.04kN) General Electric F404-GE F1D2 non-afterburning low bypass ratio turbofans

1975 **April:** Lockheed began research on the *Hopeless Diamond* project.

1975 **June:** First series of tests on the two one-third-scale wooden models of the *Hopeless Diamond* began.

1975 **September:** Scale model of *Have Blue* was built.

1975 **August:** Lockheed and Northrop invited to develop and test an aircraft known as the Experimental Survivable Testbed (XST).

1975 **1 November:** Lockheed and Northrop awarded contracts of $1.5m each to conduct phase 1 of the XST programme.

1976 **26 April:** Lockheed Development Corporation (LADC) received the go-ahead to build two *Have Blue* demonstrators (Phase 2 of the XST programme).

1976 **June:** Fabrication of the first aircraft began in Building 82 at the Lockheed Burbank, California plant.

1977 **June:** The USAF set up a Special Project Office (SPO) in the Pentagon. Its objective was to explore low-observable technology then being demonstrated in Phase 1 of the XST programme.

1977 **17 October:** *Have Blue* HB1001 completed the final assembly stage and began ground trials.

1977 **30 November:** First flight of *Have Blue* HB1001 began, piloted by Bill Park.

1978 **4 May:** HB1001 crashed.

1978 **20 July:** HB1002 made its maiden flight.

1978 **September:** F-117 proposal submitted to USAF.

1978 **16 November:** Lockheed given a contract for five full-scale development (FSD) F-117s and for twenty full-scale engineering development (FSED) aircraft under the code name *Senior Trend*.

1979 **1 January:** Construction of full-scale wooden mock-up began.

1979 **11 July:** *Have Blue* HB1002 crashed.

1979 **15 October:** Activation of the 4450th Tactical Group (TG), and the initiation of a three-phase construction programme to improve a small desert airstrip located 26 miles south-east of Tonopah in west-central Nevada.

1979 **October:** Assembly of the first FSD F-117 full serial number 79-01780, commenced at Burbank.

1981 **22 May:** 780 made its first taxi run.

1981 **11 June:** Activation of the 4450th Test Squadron (TS) – known as I-Unit at Nellis AFB and Q-Unit at Tonopah .

1981 **18 June:** First flight of FSD F-117 780, piloted by Hal Farley, the first of five full-scale development examples. It had small vertical stabilisers which were replaced after the tenth flight. The landing gear was left down for the entire 13-minute sortie.

1981 **4 July:** Maiden flight of FSD F-117 781.

1981 **17 November:** First air-to-air refuelling of an F-117 (780) by a Boeing NKC-135 Stratotanker.

1981 **18 December:** First flight of 782.

1982 **5 February:** 780 became the first F-117 to test the flying characteristics of the F-117 with its weapons door open.

1982 **22 March:** F-117 flown at night for the first time.

1982 **10 April:** 784, the fourth FSD aircraft, made its maiden flight.

1982 **20 April:** 785, the first production standard aircraft, crashed as it started to get airborne on its first flight. This was caused by incorrect wiring of the yaw sensors.

1982 **7 July:** F-117 783, became the last of the five FSDs to fly.

1982 **7 July:** The first weapons release test conducted by 781.

1982 **23 August:** 4450th TS accepted delivery of the Group's first *Senior Trend* aircraft (787) after it passed its initial set of trials at Groom Lake.

1982 **15 October:** Maj Al Whitley became the first 4450th TG operational pilot to fly the new fighter, which earned him the distinction of being the unit's first 'Bandit'.

1982 **October:** The first unguided weapon separations were made by aircraft 781.

1982 **31 December:** By this date the 4450th TS had seven F-117As on strength.

1983 **January:** Activation of 4451st Test Squadron.

1983 **July:** I-Unit formed and took the name 'Nightstalkers'.

1983 **28 October:** 4450th TG received its fourteenth aircraft (799) and the Group achieved Initial Operational Capability (IOC), only twenty-eight months after the F-117A's first flight.

1983 **14 December:** Leading edge extensions were first tested on 780 in an attempt to reduce take-off and landing speeds. The speed reduction was too small to warrant modifications to the fleet.

1983 **14 December:** F-117A 782 was painted with a unique American flag scheme for a change of command ceremony. The flag remained on the aircraft until March 1984.

1984 **October:** The US Navy evaluated the F-117A.

1985 **March:** The 4450th TG had its first Operational Readiness Inspection and achieved a rating of 'Excellent'.

1985 **11 April:** After making its final flight, the first F-117A (780) was placed in storage. It had made a total of 137 flights during its four-year test career. Later, it was put on display at Nellis AFB.

1985 **June:** Operational command of the F-117As was transferred to the Tactical Fighter Weapons Center at Nellis.

1985 **1 October:** Z-Unit formed, which became the 4453rd Test and Evaluation Squadron, known as the 'Grim Reapers'.

1986 **11 June:** Aircraft 818 became first F-117A to have its BX 199 radar absorbent coating applied by robotic spray.

1986 **11 July:** F-117A 81-10792 crashed and its pilot was killed.

1986 **September:** 10,000 flying hours on the F-117A programme achieved.

1987 **April:** 10,000 F-117A flights completed.

1987 **28 May:** 783 conducted the first demonstration of an F-117A with a Paveway III (GBU-27) bomb.

1987 **14 October:** 85-0815 crashed at a Nellis gunnery range, the pilot was killed.

1988 **10 November:** Assistant Defense Secretary J. Daniel Howard revealed a single grainy photograph of the F-117A during a Pentagon press conference.

1989 **5 October:** The 4450th Tactical Group and its subordinate units were deactivated and replaced by the 37th Tactical Fighter Wing, under the operational command of the 12th Air Force.

1989 **20 December:** Two F-117As became first of type to be used in combat, during Operation *Just Cause* in Panama.

1990 **21 April:** The public unveiling of the F-117A – two aircraft flew into Nellis AFB from Tonopah for the occasion.

1990 **21 August:** First declassified photograph of the F-117A was released.

1990 **12 July:** The 59th and last production F-117A (87-0843) was delivered at a ceremony at Lockheed's Palmdale, CA, facility.

1990 **21 August:** First 18 F-117As arrived at King Khalid AFB (KKAB) in Saudi Arabia under Operation *Desert Shield*.

1990 **4 December:** Eighteen additional F-117As of the 416th TFS arrived at KKAB.

1990 **6 December:** For the retirement of then 'Skunk Works' president Ben Rich, aircraft 831 was painted with a version of the famed skunk logo on its underside and flown over a celebration at the test site.

1991 **17 January:** The first bomb dropped by an F-117A at 02.51hrs, signalled the start of Operation *Desert Storm*.

1991 **28 February:** End of *Desert Storm*.

1991 **1 April:** Col Whitley and seven other F-117A pilots, together with 130 support personnel, were the first to arrive back at Nellis AFB to the cheers of 25,000 people after operations in the Middle East.

1991 **17 July:** F-117A 781 delivered to USAF Museum at Wright-Patterson AFB. It had accumulated 522 flying hours. All of its radar absorbent coatings had been bead-blasted off.

1992 **9 May:** 417th TFTS moved from Tonopah to Holloman AFB, New Mexico, to be followed by the other two F-117A squadrons which subsequently formed the 49th Fighter Wing at the base. Weather, air traffic reasons and airspace availability were cited as reasons for the move.

1992 **16 May:** 780 mounted on plinth for display at Nellis AFB, Nevada.

1992 **4 August:** The third operational F-117A (82-0802) was lost in a nocturnal mishap.

1993 **June:** The F-117A made its first official operational deployment to Europe, when eight aircraft flew into Gilze Rijen in the Netherlands for Exercise *Central Enterprise*. Before that,

F-117As had been shown at the Paris Air Show in 1991 (its European public debut) and Air Fete '92 at RAF Mildenhall (its first UK showing).

1994 **December:** The F-117A fleet clocked up 100,000 flying hours.

1997 **22 January:** Lockheed Martin delivered the first F-117A with the RNIP-Plus navigation system from Honeywell after it had been overhauled in Palmdale, CA.

1997 **14 September:** 793 crashed while performing at the Chesapeake Air Show at Middle River, MD. The pilot ejected safely.

1998 **October:** Phase One tests completed, which allowed a pilot to receive live threat information and replan a mission manually from the cockpit.

1999 **24 March:** F-117As led NATO's Operation *Allied Force* air strikes against Yugoslavia.

1999 **27 March:** 82-0806 was destroyed on a combat mission in the Balkans.

1999 **1 April:** The US Defense Secretary directed twelve more F-117As to join Operation *Allied Force*, in addition to the twenty-four already participating.

2001 **21 June:** Four F-117As from Holloman AFB were flown in formation over Edwards AFB in celebration of the 20th anniversary of the first flight of the F-117A.

2002 **2 April:** Development tests completed the second phase of a demonstration project designed to provide the F-117A with the ability to receive and transmit mission and target data in real time from the air.

2003 9th FS deployed to South Korea, with anxiety rising concerning the attempt by North Korea to assemble a nuclear arsenal and the relationship between that country and the US worsening.

After 24 years service F-117 #782 was retired from the 410th Flight Test Squadron in October 2005. To mark its retirement it was again painted with the American flag on its underside. (Frank Mormillo)

A pair of F-117As made their last visit to Fairford in July 2007. One aircraft took part in the flying display, while the other was lined up in the USAF 60th anniversary park.

2004 **January:** An F-117A successfully released a 2,000lb Joint Direct Attack Munition (JDAM) for the first time.

2005 **October:** The USAF made the decision to retire F-117A 782. With over 1,200 flights and 1,500 flying hours during its nearly twenty-four-year flying career, volunteers from the 410th Flight Test Squadron at Edwards AFB got together and repainted the aircraft with the American flag as a tribute to its contribution to the F-117A programme.

2005 **14 November:** 782 flew to Holloman AFB to be used as a maintenance trainer. In exchange, the 410th FLTS at Palmdale received aircraft 811 for flight test use.

2006 The integration of JDAM and other precision-guided weapons on the F-117A, and the Block II software upgrade, achieved Initial Operating Capability (IOC).

2006 A draft version of the 2006 Quadrennial Defense Review and the 2007 US defence budget were leaked. They proposed retiring the entire F-117A fleet to make room for buying more F-22A Raptors.

2006 **June:** The 25th anniversary of the type's first flight in 1981.

2006 **25 July:** The Nighthawk passed the 250,000-flying hour mark.

2006 **14 September:** New 49th FW commander Col David Goldfein flew his first F-117A and became the last 'Bandit'.

2006 **27 October:** At Holloman AFB, a gathering was held to commemorate twenty-five years of Nighthawk history at a 'Silver Stealth' ceremony. An invitation was extended to those who had been part of the programme over the years, as well as those who still contribute to the continued success of the world's first true stealth aircraft as the type neared retirement. A formation of twenty-five Nighthawks from the 49th FW passed over the Tularosa Basin.

2006 **31 December:** The 7th Fighter Squadron, the 'Screamin Demons', officially deactivated as there was no longer need for a formal training unit.

2007 **1 January:** The first ten F-117As from the 49th FW were officially retired at Holloman AFB.

2007 **12 March:** Six of the ten retired F-117As were flown to Tonopah for storage after a ceremony at Holloman AFB.

2007 **14–15 July:** Two F-117As took part in the US Air Force 60th Anniversary celebration at the Royal International Air Tattoo at RAF Fariford.

The stealth fighter's existence was such an open secret that even the USAF joked about it. At an Edwards AFB Air Show an area was roped off in the static aircraft park. It contained a ladder, wheel chocks, and an official display sign labelled 'F-19 Flying Frisbee'. Of course 'this was an invisible plane', so no one could actually see it.